The Life and Times
of Leith

James Scott Marshall

The Life and Times of Leith

JAMES SCOTT MARSHALL

Foreword by
PETER HEATLY
C.B.E., D.L.

JOHN DONALD PUBLISHERS LTD
EDINBURGH

ISBN 0 85976 128 2 (Paper)
ISBN 0 85976 148 7 (Cloth)

Exclusive distribution in the United
States of America and Canada by Humanities
Press Inc., Atlantic Highlands, NJ 07716,
USA.

Phototypeset by H.M. Repros Ltd., Glasgow
and printed in Great Britain by Bell & Bain Ltd., Glasgow.

Foreword

This book is about a town that is different and special. It tells the story of Leith from its beginnings in the little cluster of huts by the side of the Water of Leith to the important centre of commerce and industry it is today. It also succeeds in placing Leith in its proper historic setting and reminds us of the part the Port has played in many momentous events of national significance.

We are reminded of the underlying spirit of independence, too powerful to be subjugated by the yoke of feudal vassalage, which held the Port apart from Edinburgh for many generations — also of the singularly successful period which began in 1833 when Leith secured its own municipal identity and lasted until 1920.

The Life and Times of Leith provides a story of resolute enterprise pursued with that indomitable perseverance which has characterised its citizens throughout the centuries.

The author is a son and a lover of Leith. James Marshall tells me that he enjoyed writing this book. Having enjoyed his enjoyment, I can well believe him. From its pages one can sense the energy and affection that has gone into the making of a book which must have a particular appeal for all who, like myself, can claim a close connection with this great and stirring old port.

Peter Heatly C.B.E. D.L.

Preface

There is no readily available history of Leith. William Maitland and Hugo Arnot, in their histories of Edinburgh, included references to Leith, but that was the extent of their interest. Alex Campbell's *History of Leith*, published in 1827, is now hard to come by, and it has its drawbacks. Campbell blended fact and fiction, and as his work was part of the fight then being waged by Leith for independence, it was more than a little prejudiced. He has no good word to say for Edinburgh on any subject.

John Foggo, the English master at Leith High School, projected a history of Leith, and gathered notes for that purpose; but he died before realising his ambition, and his notes disappeared — not an uncommon tragedy in the realm of research.

Dr D.H. Robertson produced his *Sculptured Stones of Leith* in 1851, and this invaluable antiquarian record of Old Leith was accompanied by a historical account in four chapters, bringing the story to the end of the eighteenth century. Then in 1896 J. Campbell Irons, a Leith solicitor, brought out his two massive volumes on *Leith and Its Antiquities*, and this work is a goldmine, for he included verbatim transcripts of many of his sources. It is now almost a century since the *Antiquities* first appeared, and second-hand copies, when found, are expensive.

John Russell's *Story of Leith* is the best known and most widely read of all the histories. Russell, however, was a schoolmaster who wrote his *Story* for schoolchildren, and five-sixths of the book is concerned with the romantic period before 1707.

There is need for a general view of that richly coloured tapestry that is the history of the ancient port of Leith. A jigsaw is perhaps a more apt comparison, for in the following pages an attempt is made to present a coherent picture from many diverse pieces which all relate to one developing community. I have been indebted to many libraries and repositories all over this city for details of Leith's many-sided life, and everywhere I found courtesy and a lively interest in the work.

In particular I have been most grateful to two people. My friend Bill Cumming, in addition to his skill at the organ, has readily given me his help and advice as an outstanding amateur photographer, and he has contributed many of the photographs in this book. My wife Mary, once again, has filled the role of reader and critic, pointing out what had to be changed in the draft, and handing it back for retyping. Truly we are beholden to our friends.

J.S.M.

Contents

CHAPTER 1

The Mediaeval Village

The Foot of the Walk is the centre of Leith today, but it was not always so. Turn along Great Junction Street and stand on Junction Bridge looking downstream. Aesthetically the scene is a vast improvement on the dereliction and litter to be seen ten years ago, and from a hygienic point of view an impressive advance on the state of things at the beginning of this century. At that time the port was thriving, and this same viewpoint then included Hawthorn's engineering works on the right bank of the river, with Yooll's Wharf next to it, facing across the water to coalyard and railway on the left bank, with Innes's shipyard adjacent, and Menzies' yard further downriver. The two drawbridges at Tolbooth Wynd and Bernard Street were both at work to allow the passage of small craft up and downstream at high water. The river itself, carrying the effluent of several paper mills and other industries, to which were added the indescribable off-scourings of many businesses around the harbour, and the filth hosed through the scuppers of many ships, looked slimy and stank horribly. This was then the heart of Leith: the life of the town flowed up and down the Kirkgate, the Tolbooth Wynd and the Shore.

All that dirt and stench and overcrowding, however, only arrived and built up with the Industrial Revolution, which began to affect Leith in the latter part of the eighteenth century — a comparatively recent development when measured against the long history of the port. In the mid-eighteenth century Leith had little more than 5000 inhabitants, and was still referred to as a village. The previous two centuries had seen the population increase a bare twenty-five per cent. The reasons for that were plain enough. Most of the children born never grew up: after a bad harvest the following winter was a time of scarcity, and sometimes famine, and the poor starved. There were many bad harvests, and there were epidemics. The last outbreak of bubonic plague, in 1645, carried off almost two-thirds of the inhabitants. Given a seaport exposed to infection from abroad, and also from troops so frequently quartered in the town, a static population was not surprising.

The Vaults, Giles Street: Continuously in use for wine storage since the early 15th century.

The year 1560 was very important for Leith. In that year the port was born again. The Leith that emerged from the year of the Reformation in Scotland bore little resemblance to what had gone before, but the village that experienced a holocaust in the mid-sixteenth century was already old. Its history was no less real and exciting because there was no one to record it. Today, at the distance of several centuries, we can only piece together from scraps and hints in other writings something that may suggest a picture of the seaport at the mouth of the Water of Leith in pre-Reformation times.

There is no satisfactory derivation of the word 'Leith'. The alternatives suggested are only scholarly guesses. Originally the name could well have referred to the river. Highwater mark is retreating about a foot every year, due to the tilting of the earth, and there is a raised beach twenty-five feet above the present sea-level. As the Romans crossed the river on their way to Cramond, they may have known Inverleith as a settlement near the mouth of the Water of Leith.

Be that as it may, the first cottages erected to form what came to be known as Leith were built where the river met the Forth estuary.

Restalrig Church in Ruins: Unroofed in 1560, the church was restored, and worship resumed in 1836.

There was nothing permanent about those early biggings. Boulders from the beach, the lower courses bound together with hot lime poured over them, unwanted chinks closed with divots, and thatched with heather, or more likely with reeds — these were the materials of the original Leith. No trace of that Leith remains, but William Maitland, in his *History of Edinburgh* in 1753, mentions that ancient cluster of hovels, saying they were known as the 'Closets' or little closes. Huddled together, without any street or thoroughfare, without even an agreed building line, those first houses occupied that area later bounded by the Shore, the Tolbooth Wynd, Water Street and the Broad Wynd.

The river was broader then. The swift current was checked, as it approached the Forth, by the flats of the Links and the flowing tide. Silt accumulated along the banks, gradually narrowing the stream, and forming the bar at the river mouth that was to prove such a problem to shipping in time to come. The Shore of Leith was begun when the first inhabitants shored up the river bank to provide anchorage for their boats.

It is arguable that there could have been a settlement at Leith before there was any castle at Edinburgh. Roads in Scotland then were few and difficult, and freight was largely seaborne. The harbour at Leith was primitive, but it was none the less the gateway to the Lothians, and from an early period the port must have been busy. Coasting vessels were small; without navigational aids they did not often venture out of sight of land, and the autumn gales brought most seagoing to an end for the winter. In summer, however, longer voyages were made — to the Low Countries, the Baltic, and down the western seaboard of France and Portugal. The wine trade with Bordeaux, and the export of salt fish and hides, were established from very early times, and the first extension of the Shore must have been upriver to accommodate the wine ships as near as possible to the Vault of William Logan.

Leith lay on the lands of the de Lestalrics — a Norman family who seem to have adventured into Scotland not long after the Norman Conquest in the eleventh century. When David I made Edinburgh one of the original four royal burghs, the de Lestalrics may already have been local landowners, but all foreign trade was concentrated in the royal burghs, and although no charter survives, it was probably on its establishment as a royal burgh that Edinburgh was given possession of the harbour at Leith. But that was all; Edinburgh had no land rights in Leith. Sometime before 1382 Sir Robert Logan married Katharine, daughter of Sir John de Lestalric, and heiress to the family estates. Sir John died in 1382, and Sir Robert Logan became the laird. He soon made his presence felt as a strong and ruthless character, and in 1398 he did a deal with Edinburgh which was to prove the source of centuries of trouble for Leith. The original charter giving Edinburgh possession of Leith harbour had long since disappeared, but it had been renewed by King Robert the Bruce in 1329. This hardly satisfied Edinburgh, however: possession of the harbour was a valuable asset, but it was also important to have free access there. The de Lestalrics had been difficult to deal with — they would only allow the Edinburgh merchants one narrow route to the harbour ten feet wide (later recalled in the name of Burgess Close). Logan, in need of money, was more amenable, and he sold Edinburgh the superiority of the strip of land between the houses and the river, together with free access thereto. That was in 1398.

It must have been about this time that Sir Robert Logan sought and received permission from King Robert III to erect the port of Leith into a burgh of barony. This can only be inferred, for there is

Andrew Lamb's House: Popularly so-called. This house belongs to the early 17th century, and probably occupies the site of an earlier dwelling.

no documentary evidence of the fact. But there is no doubt that several trade incorporations existed in the port long before the Reformation — in particular the Cordiners or Shoemakers, the Tailors and the Wrights and Masons — and such corporations were only allowed to exist in burghs. Both the Cordiners and the Tailors claimed to have originated in 1398, and it is reasonable to suppose that the burgh of Leith dated from that year.

The laird's income benefited greatly from the existence of a burgh of barony on his land. Royal burghs were possessions of the Crown, and enjoyed certain rights and privileges. Foreign trade, for example, was confined to royal burghs; various market days were allowed, and members of the various incorporations had a monopoly in their trade. Every tradesman had to be a burgess, and had to reside in the burgh. The effect of all this was that trades in Scotland were confined to the burghs. When burghs of barony came to be established, they were not allowed to engage in foreign trade, but they did have the right to establish trade incorporations, and they did have markets, and petty customs which went to the laird.

Edinburgh, understandably, was incensed at the enhancement of Leith's status. The city saw it as intolerable that a burgh of barony should be permitted only a mile and a half away. The magistrates huffed and puffed, complained that the standards of Leith tradesmen were lower than those in the royal burgh, and that the rascally Leithers deliberately undercut the Edinburgh tradesmen. Leith on the other hand found it ridiculous that a seaport should be forbidden to trade abroad, and ignored this prohibition as often as possible. Both the city and the port knew the law, however, so outwardly they adapted their behaviour to make a show of conformity, but from the beginning of the fifteenth century feeling ran high between the two.

It was not long before Sir Robert Logan became aware that all was not well in his new burgh of barony. Those old corporations were not like a modern trade union. Membership included both employers and employees, masters and journeymen; and the aims of the association were more than economic. Certainly the incorporations kept a strict monopoly in their own trade; they set standards of workmanship, superintended the training of apprentices, and agreed retail prices: but above all there was a spiritual motive at work. People then lived much closer to death than they do now, and sickness and poverty were never far away. Well, there was a better life to come, provided the poor sinner could find forgiveness and acceptance beyond the grave. Those who could afford it paid for masses to be said for their souls, but that was a luxury beyond the means of a poor tradesman. An association of tradesmen, however, could share the expense of maintaining a chapel in the parish church, and a priest to attend there and pray for the souls of departed brethren and their wives and families. Unfortunately there was no parish church in the burgh of Leith, the port being but an outlying village in the parish of Restalrig. The church at Restalrig was important, for the shrine of St. Triduana attracted pilgrims from far and near. Any proposal to introduce chantry chapels there to serve the needs of the tiny Leith incorporations would hardly be entertained, especially as Edinburgh objected to the very existence of these corporations, and as far as possible ignored them. This was probably the state of affairs in Leith in the early fifteenth century. The village enjoyed burgh status, but the corporations were deprived of what they themselves saw as their most important privilege.

Against this background, Sir Robert Logan in 1430 made a surprising move, inviting canons of the Order of St. Anthony at Vienne in France to come over and set up a house of their order in Leith. Logan was by no means a religious man, and his motives in this were less than spiritual. Given the temper and outlook of the fifteenth century, the local trade associations, bereft of spiritual benefits, were not properly established. Edinburgh would be delighted to see these Leith bodies disappear. Logan's move could not fail to be an advantage to Leith; and so the Preceptory of St. Anthony was established.

The only house of its kind in Scotland, St. Anthony's was a small and poor foundation, with never more than half a dozen canons in residence. They cultivated a garden and orchard, and the later Yeardheids (or Yardheads) followed the boundary of that ancient ground. Gifts were made to the newcomers, and sundry acres in various places yielded them a small income from rents: but their main income came from wine. From every tun imported at the Shore, one quart went to St. Anthony's, either for use or sale; and in addition the wine imported at Leith was auctioned by the canons to the wine merchants of Edinburgh.

These Frenchmen became much involved with the community. They provided the only kind of care offered to the sick and aged, and they trained local boys to read and sing, that they might assist at the services in the little chapel of the Preceptory. That chapel was also a godsend to the local incorporations, who were able to worship there, contributing to the support of the canons.

By far the most numerous and wealthy of the corporations were the Mariners. Strictly speaking this was not an incorporated body — they were a Fraternity, and always referred to themselves as such. The Fraternity were older than any of the incorporations, for they claimed 1380 as the year of their foundation. The Mariners worshipped at the Preceptory, but must have found the accommodation there inadequate. At any rate in 1483 it was probably at the instigation of the sailors that the great kirk of St. Mary's began to be built. This presumption is made from the fact that St. Mary was the patron saint of the Mariners. Other corporations no doubt contributed as they were able, and the building was gradually extended. The high altar and the nave seem to have been erected first, the aisles and transepts and the great central tower being added later. The finished kirk was twice as large as the building that remains today in the churchyard between the Kirkgate and Constitution Street.

The origin of South Leith Parish Church was probably unique in Scotland. It was a guild kirk, erected and maintained by the Leith incorporations — or guilds, as they were more generally known

Carved stone — Trinity House: The Fraternity of Mariners originated in 1380. This stone was taken from their Hospital and Convening House built in 1570, which made way for the present building in 1816.

throughout Europe. Apart from the high altar to St. Mary, there was a chantry chapel to St. Barbara, another patron of the Mariners; and similar chapels dedicated to St. Matthew for the Maltmen; to the Holy Blood for the Traffickers (or Merchants); to St. Crispin for the Cordiners; to St. Peter for the Fleshers; and to St. John for the Wrights and Masons. It was an extraordinary building, when it is recalled that the parish church at Restalrig was still functioning, and that Leith then probably had less than 4000 inhabitants.

At this period North Leith was an area rather than a place. Robert Ballantyne, Abbot of Holyrood, exercised jurisdiction over lands extending to the north bank of the Water of Leith. In addition the

Holyrood lands included the area of St. Leonard's on the south side of the river. This was small in extent, reaching as far as the Vaults, but with no access over the river save by fording. Ballantyne (or Bellenden) had a stone bridge built, which remained for over three centuries. In that same year — 1493 — the chapel of St. Ninian was built at the north end of the bridge, and a group of houses were erected on the south side. A toll on the bridge, added to the rents from the houses, sufficed to pay meagre stipends to the two chaplains appointed to serve the chapel and to light the little place of worship. Some years later, and for some reason now unknown, a second chapel was built nearby, on what later became the site of the Citadel. The dedication here was to St. Nicholas, patron of travellers, but no other information on this out-station of the great lands of Holyrood Abbey is now available.

King James I realised the potential of Leith, and subscribed to the building of the Preceptory there. Shortly after, he conceived the idea of what became known as the King's Wark. He would have liked to begin shipbuilding at the river mouth, for Scotland needed a navy; but the lack of deep water, added to the shortage of money, made the idea impossible. Nevertheless the site was convenient, with fairly easy access to Holyrood, so the King had provision made there for storing ordnance, and sheltering cargoes offloaded and intended for royal use. As opportunity offered, and money became available, James and his successors elaborated on the original idea of the Wark, each sovereign in his time adding something to the growing complex of buildings, so that in time it became a conspicuous development seaward of the original 'closets' of Leith, with its boundary wall right on the beach.

The idea of a navy loomed larger with James IV than with his predecessors on the throne, and it was he, looking for prestige, who decided that as deep water could not be found at Leith, shipbuilding must begin a mile west along the coast, where a small fishing hamlet already existed. Here, then, in the first years of the sixteenth century, a shipyard was constructed, and several ships were built, the biggest and most famous of these being the *Great Michael,* launched in 1511. The village was extended with new houses to accommodate the shipyard workers, a ropewalk was set up on the links east of the village, and a chapel built and dedicated to the Virgin Mary and St. James. This chapel was a dependency of St. Anthony's at Leith.

In the end, despite the enthusiasm of those early days, Newhaven

— 'Our Lady's Port of Grace' — never became the great centre of shipbuilding James had intended. The disaster of Flodden in 1513 left the Newhaven scheme without its director and driving force. The *Great Michael* was sold, the shipyard fell idle, and the place reverted to its former status as a fishing village. But there was one significant change, for in 1510 Edinburgh bought Newhaven from King James. A condition of the sale was that the city would keep the harbour and bulwarks in good repair, and this was done through most of the sixteenth century; but thereafter neglect set in, and the wind and tide broke up what had once been well maintained. The coast between Leith and Newhaven has been subject to extensive erosion over the centuries, and Alexander Campbell, the first Leith historian, suggested that when Newhaven was first named, with the alternative title of 'Our Lady's Port of Grace', it was in fact a sheltered haven with enclosing headlands on either side, but that in time the gales and the strong undertow washed away the protective headlands, leaving the coast as it is today, without any marked indentation.

Although Edinburgh did not yet own the superiority of the whole of Leith, the city had feudal rights over the Shore and harbour, and was continually pressing her powers as a royal burgh. Not only was foreign trade prohibited to Leithers, the city tried to prevent any kind of trade being exercised in the port. Edinburgh, in fact, refused to recognise that Leith was a burgh of barony. The magistrates kept insisting that to exercise any trade a Leither must become a burgess of Edinburgh and must reside within the royalty of the city. Innumerable rules were laid down and fines imposed for their non-observance. Leith's response to all this was defiance. As far as possible the people of the port paid no attention to Edinburgh's rules, and lived and traded as they liked, paying the fines or going to prison if and when they were caught. Since it was impossible for even the most vigilant of the Edinburgh magistrates to fine or imprison the entire population of the port, Leith's misdemeanours were ignored for longer or shorter periods, until another drive against the more barefaced lawbreakers was organised.

Life in Leith then was exciting. Not only was there the constant need to beware of Edinburgh, there was little stability in international relations. From time to time the city magistrates ordered weaponshowings on Leith Links, when all able-bodied citizens had to parade with their weapons, and demonstrations were given of their proper use.

Kirkgate Tavern: This ancient hostelry, with its three-arched piazza in the Kirkgate, was removed about a hundred years ago.

After the death of James V relations with England worsened over the ambition of King Henry VIII to effect a union of the crowns of England and Scotland through the marriage of his son Edward to Mary, the infant daughter of James. Negotiations found the Scots reluctant, and Henry considered he had been deceived. His army was then engaged in France, but he sent his brother-in-law Edward Seymour, Earl of Hertford, with a fleet, to do as much damage as he could in Scotland. His orders included the following: 'Sack Leith, and burn and subvert it, and all the rest, putting man, woman and child to fire and sword, without exception, when any resistance shall be made against you'.

Hertford carried out his orders with enthusiasm. The English fleet sailed up the Forth and disembarked at Granton on Sunday 4th May 1544. Between twelve and one o'clock the English army entered Leith after only token resistance by a Scots army quite unprepared. John Knox noted that the invaders 'found the tables covered, the dinners prepared, such abundance of wine and victuals... that the like articles within the like bounds was not to be found neither in Scotland nor in England'. The obvious signs of wealth and good living in Leith were commented on by more than one observer: 'The town of Leith was found more full of riches than we thought to have found any Scottish town to have been'. The original village of Leith was still a small huddle of poor cottages, but the harbour was full of ships, for this was now the chief port in Scotland, and the adjacent land was dotted about with the homes of wealthy merchant skippers, officials with duties at the King's Wark, and some people of wealth and fashion attracted by the green and fertile land beside the river, little more than a mile from Holyroodhouse.

The English stayed for a fortnight and wrought havoc. All the shipping was either burnt and sunk, or if thought valuable enough, sent to join the English fleet. Two vessels in particular were admired and moved out to the fleet in the roads: these were the *Salamander,* a gift from the King of France at the marriage of his daughter to James V in 1537, and the *Unicorn,* one of the few gems of the Scots navy. Then they burnt the wooden pier, carried fire through all the country round about, and burnt Leith comprehensively. Lastly Edinburgh was set alight before the invaders made their way back to England on foot, leaving a trail of destruction and misery all along their way.

Revulsion at such savagery must be tempered as we realise the barbarity of those times, and that there was little to choose between the Scots and the English in their ruthless cruelty on occasion. One historian has pointed out that this same Edward Seymour was a man of humane and enlightened principles whose main fault was a hasty temper! He was impatient, apt to say things he later regretted, and prone to impetuous behaviour. Be that as it may, Leith was left in smoking ruins. Yet the disaster cannot be compared with the destruction of a city in twentieth-century warfare. In the sixteenth century it was the rich who suffered most, having most to lose. The ordinary cottager could rebuild his turf and boulder walls and re-thatch his roof without too much trouble. He owned very little furniture or other goods. When the enemy appeared, the women and children fled — and the men too, if they thought the cause was hopeless. Before long life was settling to something like normality again.

But not for long. Leith was entering a period of change and upheaval. It is doubtful if at any time in the following four centuries life in Leith could be described as humdrum and uneventful. Within a few months of the burning of the port a man appeared there — a man with a message that betokened the national and international eruption known to later generations as the Reformation. George Wishart preached the new doctrine that criticised the Church's failure to practise what it preached and advocated fundamental change. In Leith, a fortnight before Christmas 1545, Wishart preached his last recorded sermon, taking as his theme the Parable of the Sower from St. Matthew's Gospel. Shortly afterwards he was arrested and suffered a martyr's death at St. Andrews. John Knox had looked to Wishart as his mentor and exemplar, and long after Wishart had gone Knox was to know Leith well, and himself to be well known there.

King Henry VIII died in 1547, and Hertford was appointed regent of England until his nine-year-old nephew King Edward should reach his majority. By the will of King Henry, Hertford was created Duke of Somerset and given the title of Lord Protector. The common folk in England, blind to much in his character, called him the Good Duke. Within months of Henry's death the Good Duke was back in Leith, burning and looting a second time, and imprisoning several of the Scots nobility in St. Mary's Kirk. His object was to compel the Scots to agree to a betrothal between the young King Edward and the child Queen Mary of Scotland. He made himself feared, but failed in his mission, for Mary was got safely over to France, while her mother remained in Edinburgh.

Reformation had swept through Europe, and under Henry England had taken its own peculiar line. Matters had not yet come to a head in Scotland, but there was a strong movement for change there too. Against this Mary of Guise set her face, and she was a devout and strong-willed woman. In 1554 she took over as Regent from the Duke of Chatelherault, and almost at once she was planning to secure Leith as safe quarters for her French troops, on whose support she relied against the Protestant Lords. With this in view she offered to establish Leith as a burgh of barony, and in time to grant the port the status of a royal burgh. The representatives of the port jumped at this opportunity. For a century and a half the city had refused to accept Leith's claim to be a burgh of barony, presumably because there had been no charter or other document to prove the claim. A newly granted charter from the Queen Regent herself would do much to compel recognition from Edinburgh; and if Mary could come into possession of Leith, then indeed she could make the port a royal burgh. This would realise the fondest dreams of Leith seamen — the right to engage in foreign trade.

Mary's next move was to ascertain from the laird of Restalrig, who owned the superiority of Leith, whether he would sell it to her. On 30th January 1555 Leith agreed to pay £3000 Scots to Logan for the superiority of their town, and this sum was paid over in six instalments of £500. But the superiority in fact was made over to the Queen Regent, on the understanding that as soon as possible she would erect Leith into a royal burgh. In other words Leith paid £3000 as the price of obtaining equal status with Edinburgh. A few days later the Regent granted Leith the right to choose its own bailies — and that is all that Leith ever received for £3000.

In 1559 relations between the Queen Regent and the Protestant party worsened to the extent that Mary felt herself in a more dangerous situation day by day. Her support was diminishing, and she felt the urgent need for a place of safe retreat. She accordingly issued orders for Leith to be fortified, and this work began at once. A great earthen rampart was thrown up, in which were set six stone-built ports (or gates). The Sand Port was near the present Custom House; the St. Nicholas Port near the west entrance to the docks; Bonnytown Port where Bonnington Road now meets Great Junction Street; the St. Anthony Port near the Foot of the Walk; the Coatfold (Coatfield) Port sited a little north of Links Lane; and the Lady's Walk Port near the Assembly Rooms. The wall enclosed not only the 'closets', but the preceptory and the church, as well as the encampment of French troops, and a fair number of better-class timber-built houses owned by the more successful Leithers who in various ways had bettered their conditions far beyond what had contented their forebears.

The Protestant lords strongly objected to the fortification of Leith, but the work went ahead under Mary's orders. There is no doubt she valued Leith highly as a strategic retreat, and she had a house built there for her own use. It was situated in the Rotten Row (later Water Street) but has long since disappeared. Here Mary took up residence in October 1559 and remained for a month before returning to Edinburgh. All through that winter she was very ill with what appears to have been heart disease, but with extraordinary energy she remained very much in command of her situation.

The Reformation struggle came to a head in the spring of 1560 when an English army and fleet came to the help of the Protestant cause. On the evening of Palm Sunday the English and Scottish armies reached Restalrig, and next day the Siege of Leith began. An advance was made on Leith, but the earthen wall was a formidable obstacle. The pounding of artillery had small effect, so three mounds were thrown up to give the guns more elevation. Mount Falcon (Lady Fyfe's Brae), Mount Somerset (Giant's Brae) and Mount Pelham (on the west side near the later bowling green) were named after the captains of the gun crews, and from these heights the siege guns did extensive damage.

On Easter Sunday, April 14th, it is recorded: 'The people were assembled for worship, when during the celebration of high mass, and immediately before the elevation of the host, a bullet was shot through the great east window, passing right over the Altar'. In the bombardment the tower of the preceptory was demolished, and the great central tower of the church, with the chancel and transepts, was reduced to rubble. It that same month of April fire broke out in the Sheriff Brae area, and spread through many of the timber-built houses there. English snipers picked off the Frenchmen as they tried to fight the blaze, so in the end it was left to burn itself out. Siege activities continued throughout May, but early on the morning of 11th June Mary died, and hostilities were called off. The French troops withdrew on 13th July, and three days later the English army marched south. For Leith it was the end of an era. The old ways of life would be transformed. The mediaeval village had gone and would not be replaced. Even the religion of the people would be changed. Leithers had neither sought nor wished for any of these things: drastic change was imposed on them from outside; decisions were made by those who were powerful in the land, and ordinary folk had to abide the consequences.

CHAPTER 2

Ships and Shipbuilding

Although Leith in the sixteenth century was no more than a village, it was none the less the chief port in Scotland. The devastation and suffering brought by English invasion and French occupation did not alter the fact that the volume of trade passing through the port was steadily increasing. Since the latter years of the fifteenth century trade with the Low Countries in particular had been building up. This welcome development was strengthening Scotland's international ties, so it was the more unfortunate, then, that relations with Edinburgh were increasingly acrimonious. Foreign trade could be very profitable, and as this was restricted by law to royal burghs, Edinburgh was determined to exercise her rights and to prevent unlawful encroachments by Leith seamen. King James IV, however, with his vision of a Scottish navy, and with greatly extended trade in mind, had no wish to antagonise the seamen and shipbuilders of the port. Later in the sixteenth century Mary of Guise as Queen Regent, facing mounting opposition from the body of reformers, regarded Leith, occupied by French troops, as a safe retreat, and made a point of expressing her goodwill towards the port. After 1560 the situation rapidly changed. Queen Mary had Leith's charter of superiority in her possession. She knew Leith had paid for this, but she was pressed for money. Edinburgh was complaining at the cost of fortifying the city, and Mary decided to realise one of her few remaining assets. She presented the superiority of Leith to the Provost, Magistrates and Councillors of Edinburgh as compensation for their great expenses on behalf of herself and her husband Henry Darnley. That was in 1565 — ten years after Leith had paid £3000 for freedom.

Aware of the treachery involved in this transaction, Henry and Mary had a clause inserted in the contract with Edinburgh reserving the right to reclaim the superiority of Leith 'on intimation, Sabbath forenoon, with 40 days' warning, on payment of 10,000 merks Scots'. A few months later this reversion was granted by Mary, under the Great Seal, to her 'cousin and counselor' James, Earl of Bothwell. Bothwell's story is well enough known. The reversion of the superiority of Leith passed to the young James VI, who granted it to

16

Stone-carving, Newhaven: The wall of the former St. Andrew's Church Hall, Newhaven, is adorned with a delightful and appropriate series of carvings of sea shells and seaweed.

his Vice-Chancellor, Sir John Maitland of Thirlestane. Maitland's son finally sold it to the City of Edinburgh in 1604, on consideration of 10,000 merks paid him by the Council. This sealed the fate of Leith. Now the port was a permanent possession of the capital city.

In these circumstances the commercial development of Leith could only be slow and hesitant, for nothing is worse for trade than persistent ill-will. It became a kind of virtue in Leith to outwit Edinburgh. Leith merchants would board foreign vessels in the harbour and do business with the shipmasters. Cargoes could be loaded and cleared, or landed and moved off under cover of darkness.

Custom House: Now in the possession of the National Museum of Antiquities of Scotland, this splendid Georgian building dates from 1811.

All the tricks and ploys so widely practised in later smuggling times were common around the Shore of Leith in the sixteenth and seventeenth centuries, and with the sympathy and backing of the whole population the city magistrates had plenty to worry them. From time to time arrests were made and exemplary punishment was handed out, but this only exacerbated the ill-feeling between city and port.

Fishing was almost certainly the earliest activity of the settlers at the mouth of the Water of Leith, but as time passed and trade increased, the harbour was more and more given over to larger vessels so that around the Shore fishing became more peripheral, and subsidiary to the main business of the port. On the other hand Newhaven, which from 1631 was annexed to the parish of North Leith, maintained an unbroken tradition of fishing. Long before King James IV chose the place as suitable for building his projected navy, there was a fishing village here.

After the death of James IV and the collapse of shipbuilding at Newhaven, the people reverted to the fishing that had always been their mainstay. By the mid-sixteenth century the Free Fishermen's Society of Newhaven was an active organisation, and through the

Penguins for the Zoo: On board one of Salvesen's whaling ships, which made the voyage between Leith and South Georgia. A contribution to the unique colony of penguins at Edinburgh Zoo.

Trinity House: Contains a valuable collection of maritime antiquities.

years this body became to all intents and purposes the town council of the village. The Free Fishermen were never incorporated, but they were organised like an incorporation and in practice they enjoyed the rights and privileges of incorporation since every family in the village included at least one member or was related to a member.

Fishing was mainly for herring, and this was done from open, undecked boats, suitable only for coastal waters. Herring were plentiful, and a short trip from Newhaven brought the boats to the fishing grounds. There were only two complaints: one was that the Dutch, even in the seventeenth century, came over in busses, and fished the same grounds as the Newhaven men. These busses were much bigger than the local boats and took far more fish than the small Newhaven craft. With a 14 to 16 ft keel and 6 to 7ft beam, however, Newhaven boats handled well in the enclosed waters of the estuary. The second complaint was the unpredictability of the herring. After favouring the same area for years the fish would disappear without warning, trade would collapse, and no one knew when, if ever, the herring would return. This happened in 1726, when no herring could be found. Between 700 and 800 boats had been profitably employed along the east coast, but soon there were less than 100 searching fruitlessly. Still, the silver darlings always did return eventually.

From the 1770s herring were plentiful in the Forth, but in the autumn of 1794 there was an astonishing invasion by the fish. Many years later James Colston described the miracle:

> It is to the late Thomas Brown that the credit belongs for having found out this fertile source of revenue to the fishermen. The discovery was made by him quite accidentally, near Donibristle, on the northern side of the Firth, when he was fishing near the shore, with hook and line, to catch haddocks and pollies. He suddenly discovered that the waters were invaded by shoals of herrings, which could be gathered together in bucketfuls...

The glut lasted four years before the herring moved away again. James Wilson of the Free Fishermen's Society, as an old man, recalled that time from his boyhood. He remembered hundreds of boats between Bo'ness and Garvie, 'and when you were looking at them you would have thought easily to step from boat to boat across to the other side'. These boats, of course, were not only from Newhaven, but from all along the east coast.

The same James Wilson also lamented the changes he had seen, for later the boats had to travel many miles from land to find the herring,

Menzies & Co. Ltd. Shipyard 1909: The oldest shipyard in the port — in business from the 17th century.

'whereas in former times an hour, or half an hour was all that was required. Very often I have seen no sail hoist on a boat from the harbour to where the net would be set'.

Before the eighteenth century herring fishers simply shot the nets and then hauled them without moving from the spot — the boat, indeed, being anchored. By the 1720s this method was being abandoned. Now the nets were shot and the boat moved against wind and tide. This produced larger hauls, but required nets three times the size of the old ones — which was expensive. Lack of capital meant that nearly all the fishing from Newhaven was from small open boats, unsuited to sail the open seas to distant fishing grounds. On the other hand Newhaveners were not entirely dependent on herring for their livelihood, since haddock, lythe and pollack were also available not far from the coast. For most of the year, however, the main concern was oyster fishing.

The oyster scalps of the Forth had been famous for centuries, and they belonged to a variety of owners. From time out of mind the Newhaven men had enjoyed a monopoly of fishing the City of Edinburgh's scalps, which lay adjacent to others which were dredged by the men of Musselburgh, Fisherrow and Prestonpans. The city scalps seem to have been the best in the estuary, for they were often raided by 'foreigners' from Fife and the East Lothian coast. In 1741 the magistrates issued regulations to deal with this, but these rules were ineffective, and poaching continued. Matters came to a head in 1788 when there was a fight between twenty-four boats from Fisherrow and the Newhaveners, when two Newhaven boats were captured and towed into Burntisland.

This fracas led to an enquiry held by the High Court of Admiralty in 1791. Two years later the court issued judgment on the ownership of the Forth scalps, and one interesting fact emerged. Whereas the Magistrates and Council of the City of Edinburgh had the exclusive ownership of their scalps, this meant nothing unless the fishing rights were exercised — and the Newhaven men were the only citizens with the skill to dredge the scalps. But for them the city's right to the scalps would long since have lapsed. Nevertheless Edinburgh in 1815 decided to charge rent for the scalps, and demanded £25 from the Society of Free Fishermen.

The Society paid, but later they regretted this quiet acceptance of the charge, for Edinburgh, realising this was an untouched source of income, increased the rent repeatedly, until by 1839 the fishermen were paying £74 a year for a right which for centuries they had exercised freely by common consent. Still not satisfied, the city council now leased the scalps to an Englishman, George Clark, for ten years at an annual rent of £600! This municipal greed killed the goose that laid the golden eggs. Clark had no intention of losing out on his bargain. He brought sixty boats from England to work over the scalps from dawn to dusk every day, apparently trying to strip the beds bare. The Newhaven boats resisted, and doggedly refused to budge from their traditional grounds. Clark lost patience, refused to pay the rent, and took himself off. But his bad example seems to have infected others, for over-fishing of the beds from then on gradually destroyed the once-famous Forth oyster scalps.

The Newhaven oyster-woman's cry of 'Caller ou!' was remembered in popular song long after it had ceased to be heard in the streets of Edinburgh, but the 'dreg song' or oyster song of the men was forgotten much more quickly. There was a saying that you had to sing to the oyster to get it into the net. When working over the scalps the dredges were pulled along the sea-bed at an angle of about 45 degrees. This operation required the boat to move steadily, and a stiff breeze supplied the best motive power. Lacking enough wind, the men took the oars, and singing the dreg song kept them going smoothly together.

Henry Robb's Drawing Office: This firm, the last survivor of all the yards, built small to medium craft for specialised purposes.

Oyster dredging occupied the winter months, and during the close season from early April to mid-September the summer herring 'drave' stretched through July and August. Late spring and early summer could be filled in with a trip to Shetland for cod and ling, but for the younger, hardier, more adventurous men, a far more attractive ploy was the Greenland whaling. This had had a long history. The first evidence of whaling from Leith dates from 1615 when James VI granted a 19-year monopoly to Sir George Hay and Sir Thomas Murray in whale fishing. The object then, and for long afterwards, was whale-oil, used in the manufacture of soap — an industry then being projected for Leith. For a long time thereafter there would seem to have been no regular whaling, although expeditions were mounted from time to time. The real start of whaling as an industry at Leith came with the establishment of the Edinburgh Whale Fishing Company, whose ship the *Trial*, of 333 tons, was fitted out for Greenland fishing in 1750.

The annual sailing of the whalers from Leith in April soon became a great local event. Crowds lined the quays and pier to watch the full-rigged ships, each manned by forty or fifty men, and to cheer them clearing out of the harbour. They returned any time between late June and the end of August. In later years longer trips were made beyond Greenland into the Davis Strait, but the earlier vessels were not specially built for whaling. The *Trial*, for example, was simply a cargo vessel with bows strengthened to withstand the pressure of ice. The catches were often derisory. The *Royal Bounty* returned to Leith at the end of June 1754 with ten whales, which was reckoned extraordinary. Five or six carcases were considered a good season's fishing, and it was not unusual for a ship to return without having sighted a single whale. As there were no facilities on board for preserving or processing the catch, ships would turn for home after a good run without waiting for a full cargo.

This kind of whaling ceased to be profitable, and declined at Leith in the 1840s, although Christian Salvesen & Sons, after continuing to operate whaling stations in Shetland and Newfoundland, showed enterprise in pressing the Government for a licence to operate in the Antartic. In 1908 an expedition began work at Leith Harbour in South Georgia, and for the next half-century the whaling industry grew and prospered in the South Atlantic, with annual sailings from Leith. This was a very different business from the old Greenland whaling. Factory ships made longer trips and much bigger catches possible, and modern methods of processing practically every part of the carcace produced larger financial returns. Until the 1950s many a young Leither was able to finance his marriage from the money he could make on a whaling trip to South Georgia, where he worked hard, earned good wages, and had little opportunity for spending what he earned.

The strong element of risk in whaling always appealed to certain men, but in the old Greenland whaling there was also glamour, for those whalers were among the largest vessels ever seen in Scotland — larger than many ships which then crossed the Atlantic, and far bigger than anything ever built at Leith. Shipbuilding was an ancient skill in the port, but with no dock available it was only possible to build small craft. Nothing over 100 tons was built at Leith before 1700, although several firms are known to have been at work. In the 1720s John Young, Peter Robertson and James Beatie were all in business as shipbuilders. They each built up to 100 tons, but most of their time was spent on vessels between 12 and 50 tons. By the end of

A Ramage and Ferguson Yacht: This firm had a wide reputation as builders of luxury yachts. This is the twin-screw motor yacht *Naz Perwer* built c.1930 for H.H. Prince Youssouf Kamal of Egypt.

the century ships of 200 and 300 tons were being built, and five shipbuilding firms were at work, employing between them 152 carpenters. Yet the facilities for shipbuilding were minimal — two dry docks and nothing else — owing to the extremely parsimonious attitude of the City of Edinburgh, who owned the Shore and Harbour of Leith.

Despite the small scale of these operations there was never any lack of local pride:

> Yesterday was launched at Mr Robert Drybrough's dock at Leith, a very fine new ship, built for the service of the revenue of Excise, thought by good judges to be the most elegant in point of construction and shape, ever built in Scotland...

Thus the *Edinburgh Evening Courant* in November 1764. While the vessels built at Leith were small, that is what was in demand to serve the coastal trade. The dreadful state of the roads in Scotland ensured shipping companies a virtual monopoly of heavy freights, so the bulk of the business in and out of Leith harbour was done by small coastal craft. This state of affairs did nothing to encourage speed and efficiency, and the operation of the Forth ferry service may serve as an example of the way shipping business was conducted in the eighteenth century.

The ferry sailed between Leith and Kinghorn, and two types of craft were engaged on this run. The so-called 'Big boats' carried horses, cattle and general freight, as well as passengers; and the small pinnaces — no more than 6 or 7 tons — carried passengers only. This was a brisk trade which for many years continued without any regulations governing it. The pinnace fare was 6d (2½p), and this was a comparatively dependable service. A 'Big boat', especially in summer, might get the chance of a profitable cargo for some other part of the coast, and would at once abandon the ferry run and go off, leaving the ferry service with one less ship for the transport of heavy goods. Another complaint was that pinnace owners often overloaded their boats far beyond the safety limit; but they answered by pointing out that Big boats did not sail at all until they had loaded not only their freight, but also what the skipper thought were sufficient passengers. There had indeed been serious accidents with overcrowded pinnaces, and something would have to be done to make the Big boats more dependable.

In 1773 the Town Council issued regulations for the ferry boats, but these were condemned by all parties as unfair, ridiculous and unworkable. Pinnaces were restricted to six passengers each, and the fare was raised to tenpence. Three Big boats were ordered to sail every hour. Packmen in particular were furious, for previously they had been accounted passengers with the right to cross on the pinnaces; the new rules made them, or rather their packs, freight, restricted to using the more expensive and unreliable Big boats. Arguments, protests and petitions continued for months, and the outcome does not appear; but enough evidence remains to show the poor standards of administration and service in the ferry business.

By the end of the century the Turnpike Road Acts had produced a great improvement in the state of the roads, and the stagecoach to London was proving a strong rival to the sea voyage. The coach was uncomfortable and the journey a mixture of boredom and danger, but the searoute conformed to no timetable. It was not unusual for a ship to make a fast trip from the Thames to the Forth in under forty-eight hours, only to be delayed off the Isle of May for a week waiting for a favourable wind before making the harbour at Leith. The answer to this challenge was the introduction of the Leith smacks, which were first put on the London run in 1791 by the Leith and Berwick Shipping Co. who in that year moved their headquarters from Berwick to Leith. The smacks were almost contemporaneous with the stagecoaches. The coaches were in business for roughly half a century, before being overtaken and replaced by the railway: the smacks in rather less than that time were ousted by the steamers.

S.S. GOTHLAND

S.S. Gothland: Built by Henry Robb in 1932 to trade between Leith and Hamburg. Served as a rescue vessel during the Second World War. Her red ensign now hangs in South Leith Parish Church.

In their day the smacks were thought to be the last word in sailing achievement. Before the wind they were first-class performers, but in adverse conditions they made a much poorer showing, rolling and pitching to the great discomfort of the passengers. Nevertheless they were the pride and joy of Leith, and the times taken from the Forth to the Thames and *vice versa* were regularly published in the newspapers, and followed with the same enthusiasm as later attached to the tea clippers on the China run. Everything was done to facilitate the swift clearance of the smacks from the harbour. Harbour dues were allowed to stand over for a month or more, instead of having to be settled at the start of each voyage. In an action raised by the Dock Commissioners against Edinburgh Magistrates it was said in evidence:

> The Harbour-master had instructions from the Collector to allow smacks to pass out of the old harbour without a ticket, that they might run no risk of detention by the delay in applying for tickets, and thereby incur the danger of losing the tide. But to no other vessel was that privilege granted.

The smacks were not cargo boats, and their success was not mirrored in the general business of the port. A growing volume of industry in the town produced increasing demand for shipping services, but there was an almost complete lack of dock and harbour facilities. This was a

27

sore point in Leith for many years. A news item from the *Edinburgh Evening Courant* in July 1750 illustrates the point:

> Sunday the *Janet* of Edinburgh struck on the Bar, in coming in to the Harbour of Leith, but Yesterday Afternoon was brought up to the Key without receiving any Damage. She is upwards of 700 Tons Burden, and the largest that has ever been in that Harbour.

Admittedly something had been done. After much pressure the Town Council had applied to the Government of Queen Anne for permission to build 'a wet and dry dock for building, fitting and carining (careening) H.M. ships of war', and in 1720 the first dry dock in Scotland was opened. It was sited between the later Sandport Street and the river. Later in the century a second dry dock was built a little further upriver adjacent to the old parish kirk of North Leith. Many ships then anchored above the Coalhill, for there was ten to twelve feet of water in the channel at spring tide.

But the harbour bar prevented many ships making the harbour except at high water, and berthing facilities were so meagre that expensive delays in loading and unloading cargo were unavoidable. An Act of Parliament was obtained in 1787 for improving the harbour, but all that resulted was the building of a drawbridge at the foot of Tolbooth Wynd, replacing the old Leith Brig which had spanned the river at St. Ninian's Church since 1493. Eighteen years later another drawbridge was built at Bernard Street, and these were known as the Upper and Lower Drawbridges. A second Act of Parliament empowered the Town Council to make wet docks, dry docks, piers and quays westward from the harbour towards Newhaven, and so in 1806 the East Old Dock was opened, and the West or Queen's Dock in 1817. These were built to the plans of John Rennie, who also designed a third dock, much larger than the first two, which was intended to extend to Newhaven, where a deepwater entrance would be found; but lack of money aborted this project. As it was, Government loans for the two docks constructed amounted to £302,290 — a colossal sum for those days.

Another great drag on the expansion of trade at Leith was the multiplicity of port charges. These included Anchorage and Beaconage, Flagage and Light Dues, Lyage dues and Rowage, the 'merk per ton', Prime Gilt, Shore dues, Tonnage duty, Gold Penny, Birthage, Bulkage, Ballast dues, Pilotage — and after the drawbridges were built there was added Pontage, and with the erection of warehouses at the new docks, Shed duties. Indignation in

H.M.S. Windrush: Frigate built by Henry Robb, 1943. Presented to the Free French and renamed *L'Aventure.*

Leith had simmered for long, and the end of the French war brought a more vocal and strident note to the grumbling. What happened to all the money paid in dues? The last straw was a proposal from Edinburgh to turn the ownership of the harbour and docks over to a joint-stock company to be created for the purpose. This confirmed Leith's long-held suspicion that the proceeds of the innumerable port charges, instead of being applied for the improvement of the harbour and docks, were simply being pocketed by Edinburgh as profit. Fortunately the proposal came to nothing, and a more sensible move was the creation of a Dock Commission in 1826. The twenty-one Commissioners were made up from:

   6 members of the town council of Edinburgh
   2 merchants of Edinburgh (nominated by the town council)
   The Master of the Merchant Company of Edinburgh
   9 commissioners immediately connected with Leith
   3 commissioners appointed by the Admiralty.

The Lord Provost was *ex officio* chairman, with a deliberative and a casting vote. The Corporation of Edinburgh remained the proprietors and continued to levy all the hated dues. It was soon plain that this arrangement fell somewhat short of perfection, and changes were made from time to time. After the amalgamation of Leith and Edinburgh in 1920 the Commission consisted of 15 members — 6 elected by those paying dock rates, 3 chosen by the shipowners, 3 selected by the town council, and one each from Edinburgh Chamber of Commerce, Edinburgh Merchant Company, and Leith Chamber of Commerce. This arrangement lasted until the creation of the Forth Ports Authority, which superseded the Dock Commission.

Leith at last achieved independent status in 1833, and this fact, added to the setting up of the Dock Commission, led many Leithers to suppose that trade at the docks would soon improve. In the 1830s shipping was languishing. There were plenty of vessels to be seen, and there was much activity around the harbour, but it was only the coastal trade that was flourishing: foreign business was in the doldrums. The Baltic trade had largely left Leith in favour of Aberdeen, Dundee and Kirkcaldy, and the tidal harbour, with the harbour bar, resulted in very little of the new steamer trade coming to Leith. There was an almost universal opinion in the town that the main deterrent to maritime prosperity was the heavy port charges, and that the new Dock Commission was overloaded with Edinburgh people. This popular view was challenged by William Marshall who in 1836 published an economic analysis of the shipping trade showing that the main trouble at the port of Leith was inefficiency, and a stubborn refusal to change traditional practices.

Queen Victoria visited Scotland in 1842. For centuries royal visitors had set foot in Scotland at the Shore of Leith, but on this occasion it was decided to bring the royal yacht to anchor at Granton, where there was deep water, rather than attempt to berth at Leith, where the harbour bar could only be crossed within an hour of high water, which was at 11 p.m. on the day in question. The Provost, Magistrates and Council of Leith were mortified, and perhaps it was this public humiliation that spurred the Dock Commission into action. Six years later work was started on the construction of a new basin, and in 1851 the Victoria Dock was opened. At the same time the harbour was much improved. Extensive dredging made the water six feet deeper at the harbour bar, the East Pier was extended, and a new pier, the West Pier, was constructed, almost a mile long, carrying a railway line, and giving a reasonable depth of water even at low tide.

By this time many changes were taking place as shipowners learned to face the challenge of the new world of commercial rivalry and competition. Trade began to pick up in the late 1840s, and when the new dock was opened it was already plain that it was not big enough to meet the demand for accommodation. Before long the planners were again at work. An area east of the harbour — part of the famous Leith Sands — was reclaimed, and in 1869 the Albert Dock was completed. In the autumn of that same year Mr D.R. Macgregor, a Leith shipowner, sent two of his vessels, the steamers *Leith* and *Stirling*, to the Far East via the Suez Canal within a few days of its

Graving Dock: The first graving dock to be built in Scotland, dating from 1720. It was sited between Sandport Street and the river, but is now filled in.

opening. The Albert Dock was followed in 1881 by the Edinburgh Dock, and that in turn by the Imperial Dock in 1903. Each successive basin was larger than its predecessor, and from the mid-nineteenth century there was steady expansion in the volume of trade handled at the port. Some indication of this may be gleaned from the revenue of the Dock Commission during that period. In 1839 this amounted to £17,000; thirty years later it had increased to almost £59,000; and by 1893 the Commission's income had risen to £91,101, despite large reductions in rates charged for goods and vessels in 1883 and 1885.

Shipbuilding also advanced. It took fully a generation to convince some owners that steam would permanently replace sail. Steamers were faster and more reliable, but they were also more expensive than sailing ships, they needed larger crews, and they had an insatiable appetite for coal, which also added to costs. Nevertheless the steamer *Sirius* was launched from Menzies' yard in 1837, and was the first steamship to cross the Atlantic. Menzies could pride themselves on being in the forefront of British shipbuilders. *Sirius* was followed four years later by *R.M.S. Forth* of 1940 tons — then the largest ship ever to have been built at Leith. But it was well past the middle of the century before the last sailing ships with wooden hulls were launched from Leith yards. The later years of the century saw the establishment of several new shipyards, each inclining to its own specialty — coastal craft, general-purpose traders, larger vessels for the Far Eastern and Australia trade, while Messrs Ramage and Ferguson acquired a widespread reputation for luxury yachts.

There were ups and downs, good years and bad. The South African War was followed by a ten-year depression from 1901 to 1911. Too many ships competing for the world's trade made for much unemployment in Leith in Edwardian times. Trade was just picking up again when the First World War quickly brought all the shipyards to working at full stretch again. The post-war recession, however, saw one after another of the yards closing down until there was but one survivor — Henry Robb Ltd., a newcomer to the business, for this firm had only begun operations in April 1918. Robb's took over the two adjacent yards of Cran and Somerville, and Ramage and Ferguson. Other firms, no longer building ships, continued as ship repairers. Messrs Menzies & Co., and James G. Marr & Son continued in this role till after the Second World War, but by the time Henry Robb Ltd. closed in 1983, they had been the only firm regularly building ships at Leith for forty-eight-years. In the sixty-five years of its existence this firm built 530 craft of various specialised types — cargo liners, crane barges, rescue tugs, naval frigates, ferry boats and tankers, for firms all over the world.

Trade in and out of Leith survived the Depression of the inter-war years. The principal export was always coal, with grain and timber the main imports, largely from America and the Baltic. But the labour force was greatly reduced from the pre-1914 level, and persistent massive unemployment marked Leith as one of the industrial black spots of the 'twenties and 'thirties. The most significant development in the docks since 1945 has been rapid and extensive spread of automation. Deepwater facilities have been increased by land reclamation. Flourmills have been built where bulk grain-carriers berth, and the entire process of converting grain in the hold into flour in the bag is supervised by a handful of men. Cargoes of all kinds are now handled by a small fraction of the labour force once required for the operation, and more and more cargoes are containerised.

One result of these developments is that the dock area now has a deserted appearance compared with the bustling scenes of former days. This is deceptive: the port handles a great deal of business today, and shows a profit. Under modern conditions the work that formerly required the labour of hundreds is now within the capacity of dozens.

CHAPTER 3

Trade and Industry

The peculiarity of Leith's situation as a burgh of barony only a mile and a half from the royal burgh and capital city of Edinburgh was a constant source of irritation to the capital. All burghs had the power to establish incorporations. These were monopolistic bodies, and without membership in the appropriate corporation no man could exercise his trade. This was normally understood and accepted without question, but in Leith the situation was not so straightforward. Edinburgh had disapproved of the port's burghal status from the start and had consistently ignored the corporations there. But Edinburgh could do no more than disapprove, until the opportunity of acquiring the superiority of the port was presented by Queen Mary's financial difficulties. When this splendid prize was handed to Edinburgh in 1565, Leith's situation was considerably worsened. Edinburgh made no sudden move, as it was still possible that the superiority might be purchased back, but in 1604, as we saw (see p. 17), the city managed to buy the reversion for a payment of 10,000 merks, and from that date all of Leith, except for the area of St. Anthony, belonged to Edinburgh. The city magistrates then assumed that Leith's status as a burgh of barony was nullified, and the people of the port must be made to understand this as soon as possible. Surprisingly this assumption was not challenged in court until 1734, when judgment went against the magistrates of Edinburgh.

Within Leith itself no one questioned the legality or power of the incorporations, and every family in the village was connected with one or other of these bodies. In the small community of Leith, moreover, the same small group of men were not only officials in the incorporations, but also elders and deacons in the parish kirk. In 1593 they made themselves responsible for the stipend of a second minister in the kirk, and to all intents and purposes the kirk session, with the officials of the incorporations, acted as a kind of town council.

Workers in the same trade preferred living together in the same district. Thus the cordiners or shoemakers all lived in Calton, at the southern end of the parish of South Leith. The maltmen were mostly

The King's Wark: The original Wark being destroyed by fire in the 1690s, this tenement was shortly afterwards erected on the site.

to be found in the Yardheads, where an underground stream joining the Water of Leith gave them access to water for brewing. Shipmasters and seamen naturally favoured the vicinity of the Shore. After the Reformation, in church, the old chantry chapels were retained by the various corporations, who each provided seats there for their officials, where they sat importantly with their families while the rest of the congregation either stood or brought their own stools.

An important development took place when, about 1620, the King James Hospital was built in the south-west corner of the churchyard. This was another link between the church and the trades. Towards

Leith Bakers: In traditional dress, and carrying their banner, the Bakers prepare to join Leith Hospital Pageant.

the end of the sixteenth century the funds of the former preceptory of St. Anthony were passed to the kirk session on condition that the money would be used to continue the work formerly undertaken by the canons of the preceptory. The hospital was an eventide home for the aged poor of the corporations. Here a dozen or so old women were provided with bed, board and candle. The mariners were not included, for they had their own hospital for their sick, poor and aged in their Fraternity House (colloquially called Trinity House).

These old trade bodies bore no resemblance to trade unions. Employers and employees, masters and journeymen, were all members. When an apprentice qualified as a journeyman he became a freeman of his incorporation by paying his 'upsett' or entrance fee. Thereafter he paid quarterly contributions, and in return, if he became sick or disabled, the society paid a small pension. If necessary his funeral expenses were paid and his widow received a pension. If his son were intelligent — 'a lad o pairts' — the incorporation would nominate him for a place at the Grammar School, and pay his fees. The kirk session and incorporations were closely associated in community welfare, for the elders too paid pensions to the poor, but not if the pensioner was already a beneficiary of an incorporation. The kirk session were also the governors of the Grammar School, and saw to it that promising poor boys were given places there.

The mariners were the largest and wealthiest of these societies. The traffickers or merchants included a great variety of members, since anyone not eligible to join the mariners, maltmen or trades was accepted by the traffickers on application; and of all the corporations the traffickers were the most businesslike in their handling of funds. The maltmen also included brewers, vinegar-makers, some merchants and doctors — but no lawyers. For no stated reason lawyers were expressly barred. There were nine trade incorporations — usually acting together as a kind of federation and known as the Trades. These were the coopers, tailors, weavers, baxters, cordiners, hammermen, wrights, barbers and fleshers. These were small societies, and acted together as the Trades of Leith under the direction of a Deacon Convener.

The antipathy of the maltmen towards lawyers may have stemmed from their experience in the seventeenth century. In 1619 the Edinburgh magistrates accused them of behaving as though they were an incorporation, annually electing a deacon and admitting their own freemen. These practices, said the magistrates, were illegal, and must stop. It was true that under an Act of Parliament of 1567 maltmen were forbidden to be organised as an incorporation. This odd piece of legislation had either been forgotten or ignored, but in 1619 the magistrates compelled Leith maltmen to pay £6.13.4 for the privilege of belonging to their own society — which fee was appropriated by the Town Council as general revenue. The maltmen none the less survived and were eventually acknowledged as an incorporation by the Privy Council.

Apart from the mariners, traffickers, maltmen and trades there were the carters, the porters and the metters and weighers, who each operated independently, but when expedient, the carters allied themselves with the maltmen, and the porters and metters with the traffickers. The carters were much in the public eye, from the nature of their occupation. Originally they were sledders, for when there were few made roads, runners were better than wheels. In the mid-seventeenth century they sought permission from the magistrates to replace the runners with wheels, and so become carters. They had a numerous membership, and rented the grazing on the Links for over a hundred horses. From time to time they were pressed into service

Leith Carters: Exhibiting the best set of harness in the Carters' annual show, c. 1910.

on one side or the other in national emergencies. This happened in 1648 when Leith carters were forced to help the army of the Engagers. Later they were publicly rebuked in the kirk for this, but they had had no choice. A few years later they had to carry materials for the Cromwellian troops building the Citadel. In 1679 again, the carters were made to serve the army of the Duke of Monmouth marching to defeat the Covenanters at Bothwell Brig; and they were involved in assisting the rebels in both the '15 and '45 Rebellions. These were all unpopular causes in Leith, but pressed men have no choice if they value their lives.

The carters owned a piece of land immediately north of the churchyard in the Kirkgate, and here they erected two tenements facing the Kirkgate and Coatfield Lane. These tenements enclosed the carters' garden, where they built a convening-house in 1726. Forty years later part of the 'yaird' was leased to the Antiburghers — a group who had left the parish kirk in 1740 to form a seceding congregation. A small church was built, and the convening-house was used as a session-house. Later the convening-house was taken down and rebuilt while the church was enlarged.

The porters were an ancient body. Before the Reformation they had been known as the pynours, then later they were the 'Corporation of Workemen of South Leith'. It was only in the eighteenth century that the workmen became porters, and their work was varied. They were general porters in the streets; they were scavengers, so far as any scavenging was ever carried out; they were dockers who handled cargoes; they were removal men and undertakers. They worked in gangs or companies, each group specialising in one type of work. The full complement was twelve men to each company, and for many years there were four companies, handling wine, sugar, meal and so forth. The nineteenth century saw several more companies of porters formed to handle the increasing trade at the docks.

The metters were originally a branch or division within the Society of Porters, but by the mid-seventeenth century they were recognised as independent. They measured what was bought and sold, and in one respect they were unique in Leith, for from the earliest times they were recognised by the Edinburgh magistrates, who in fact appointed them. On appointment the metter was required to swear to be honest, and they were usually designated as Sworn Metters. Another distinguishing feature was that from very early times women as well as men were sworn in to this craft.

The Industrial Revolution destroyed the trade incorporations. The rapid rise in population made it fairly easy for an incomer to the town to work at his trade without bothering to join any incorporation. Several corporations from time to time took these 'pirates' to court, but it was soon realised that this was a waste of money, as the number of such 'unfree' tradesmen was increasing almost every month. Another troublesome development was the large increase in the number of King's freemen. Men who had served in the armed forces, and who from age or disablement were no longer fit to serve, were discharged and left to fend for themselves. No pensions were paid, but ex-servicemen who thought themselves able to work at a trade were allowed to do so without joining an incorporation. It was expensive for an outsider to join any incorporation, so permission to dispense with this was equivalent to a large sum of money to the old soldier or sailor. The corporations never complained about this privilege granted to ex-servicemen, but after the Battle of Waterloo the army and navy were drastically cut, and Leith was suddenly flooded by King's freemen, taking work from the incorporations.

Apart from all that, however, a new climate of opinion developed with the growing industrialisation of the town. The incorporations were based on the mediaeval desire for monopoly and exclusiveness;

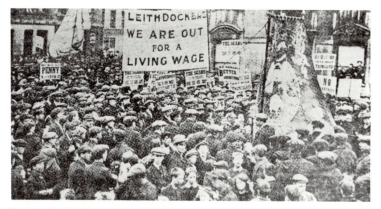

Dock Strike 1913: Industrial trouble before the First World War.

the new world of commercial rivalry and competition had no place for the exclusive rights and privileges of the Trades. Finally the Burghs Trading Act of 1846 did away with the old advantages so highly prized formerly, and for the most part the incorporations ceased to exist. The carters continued as a Friendly Society, the traffickers had already converted themselves into the Leith Chamber of Commerce. The mariners had become incorporated at the end of the eighteenth century when they began licensing pilots in the Forth, and they continued with this work. The porters were unaffected in their work patterns, continuing in companies as before; and the metters and weighers were still sworn in. The maltmen and the trade societies on the other hand simply wound up their affairs and ceased to be.

In the early nineteenth century the largest employers in Leith were the ropewalks and the glassworks, but in the widespread industrial depression following the end of the French wars, both of these enterprises were in decline. Rope- and sailmaking had had a long history in the area. There was a tradition in Newhaven that King James IV, in establishing a dockyard there, had included a ropework in his plans. This would have been reasonable, but there is no evidence of it. The first reliable indication of the existence of this industry dates from 1638, when Patrick Wood got a tack of ground east of Newhaven, on the links and shore. Wood seems to have carried on business there, for in 1663 the ground was taken by James Davidson 'for a ropeworks such as the late Patrick Wood had'.

Davidson and his brother Sir William Davidson were together

granted a monopoly of ropemaking in Scotland, but they were not interested in making ropes. The monopoly was a financial asset, which they sold to James Deans, a Canongate bailie, granting him tack of the site for £20 a year. Deans and his son tried ropemaking, but the business failed, and in 1682 the monopoly ran out. The Town Council then received an application from Jean Debaut for the use of a piece of ground between the Sand port and the Citadel port 'mentioning that he is resolved to set up a work for making rigging for ships'. This was a better site adjacent to the shipyards of North Leith; but ten years later Thomas Deans, a second son of old James, applied for a tack of the old site at Newhaven. He was granted tack for his lifetime and twenty-five years beyond.

There may now have been rumours of increasing demand for rope, for Patrick Archibald, newly returned to Leith after long residence abroad, was given permission to begin ropemaking. Deans then approached the Privy Council for a monopoly, but he was only partly successful. Foreign ropes were prohibited, but there would be no objection to other local ropemakers competing with Deans. That was in 1694, and the following year the Scottish Parliament granted a charter to 'The Company of Scotland trading to Africa and the Indies'. This was the birth of the Darien Scheme, and the fitting out of vessels brought work to the Leith ropemakers. Nor did the collapse of the Darien venture bring the Company of Scotland to an end. In September 1699 the Company fitted out the *African Merchant*, 170 tons burden, for trading to Africa, and the bill for the fitting out came to £543.13.10, of which £234.18.1 went for sails and rigging.

At the start of the eighteenth century, then, there was no lack of ropemakers in Leith, although local shipbuilding and repairing was not on a scale to support a large industry. In 1710 ropemaking moved into South Leith when John Gilmour and Thomas Mayo got tack of a site there 'near the Saw-mill'. This identifies it as the same site on which ropemaking continued during the following two centuries and more. Then in 1727 David Deas applied for a long lease of the ropework in North Leith. Deas is probably the same as Deans, and David was either the son or nephew of Thomas Deans who got tack of the Newhaven ropework in 1692. The tack now granted was for 'the Rope Work in North Leith and the Links of Newhaven', which appears to refer to both the Newhaven site and the ropework at the Citadel, which, in fact, seems to have been mainly devoted to sailmaking. By 1742 the three ropeworks at Newhaven, the Citadel, and in South Leith were all in possession of David Deas — or 'Captain Daies & Co.'

Eight years later the Town Council considered an application for a feu and tack of part of Leith Links submitted by Bailie James Mansfield and Partners, who wanted the ground for a Rope and Sail Duck factory. Mansfield 'and Partners' appear to have joined the Deas business, bringing with them much-needed capital. At the end of 1750 an announcement appeared, making it plain that the firm was now the Leith Roperie Company, with the business concentrated on the Links:

> Whereas the Roperie and Sail-cloth Coy of Leith have removed all their Stock to their Factory in the Links of South Leith, to prevent Mistakes, it is desired that their Friends will address their Commissions to David Deas or James Hutton their Managers, and to them only. At the above Factory may be had White Ropes of all Sizes, four and three Head Drest Hemp and Lint Tow at the lowest Prices.

The sail-cloth factory at the Citadel was offered for sale; the Newhaven site was retained, but probably only for storage until the tack ran out.

A few months later a second party applied to make rope on the Links, and were accommodated with a site immediately south of the Leith Roperie's ground. The two ropewalks were separated by a strip of ground twenty-four feet wide, intended as a roadway, but that project did not materialise then. This second feu was taken by the Edinburgh New Roperie Coy, which appeared to prosper from the day of its inception. By 1757 it was employing almost 400 persons. If the Leith Roperie was a comparable employer of labour, then ropemaking was certainly the principal employment of Leithers in the mid-eighteenth century, apart from seafaring. The main outlet for sails and rigging was the whaling industry, demanding the highest quality of cordage and sailcloth. Edinburgh Roperie and Sailcloth Co. continued in business for the next two centuries.

Leith Roperie Company had more of a struggle, owing to lack of capital rather than want of business. In 1763 the Company borrowed £500 from the Traffickers, and sought further loans until in 1778 their debt to the Traffickers totalled £800. As that incorporation always approved the loans without demur, it was presumably considered a worthwhile investment in a prospering business. The Leith Roperie Company was dissolved in 1848, mainly in consequence of the abandonment of the Greenland whaling.

The other great shore-based industry in eighteenth-century Leith was glassmaking. This work began in 1663 when Robert Pape built a glasshouse at the Citadel and advertised his venture in the *Kingdom's Intelligencer,* the first newspaper to be printed in Scotland — another project housed at the Citadel:

> A Remarkable Advertisement to the Country and Strangers. That there is a Glass-house erected on the Citadel of Leith, where all sorts and quantities are made and sold at the prices following... Better stuff and stronger than is imported.

At that time all glass had to be imported to Scotland, and it was dear. Pape made all kinds of glass except window glass, and had high hopes. But his business failed. For some reason now impossible to discover there seemed to be a prejudice against him. Local merchants continued to import all their glass. To add to Pape's worries, his cashier absconded with a large sum of money. Pape appealed to the Privy Council, who reaffirmed the monopoly, and forbade the import of all but window glass. But the business did not pick up and no more is heard of it.

A group of five partners now moved in at the Citadel. Only one of these was a businessman — Sir James Stanfield of Newmills — the others providing capital. This new attempt began in 1678, and the difficulties attending glassmaking in Scotland now became plain. This was a highly skilled craft, and there were no native Scots with qualifications. It would be necessary to persuade English journeymen to leave well-paid jobs and come to Scotland to teach men in Leith how to take business away from the English firms.

The nearest source of skilled workmen was Newcastle, and after many months of negotiations some men were engaged; but their work was poor (it was suspected to be deliberately poor), and they ran up debts in Scotland which Stanfield had to pay, to retain their services. Eventually the other partners had had enough, and demanded their money back. The Citadel glasshouse was closed in 1681, and the whole concern — buildings and equipment — was sold by public roup. At the roup Sir James Stanfield and Sir Robert Gordon of Gordonstoun bought the business between them. Alexander Ainslie was engaged as manager, and with more men from Newcastle production started again. But trouble seemed to cling to the enterprise. Stanfield was murdered in November 1687, and the trial and execution of his son for that crime was a *cause célèbre.*

Hawthorn's Yard: Hawthorn built both ships and railway engines. A view from the turn of the century.

Glassmaking now made a fresh start under quite a different type of management. Ainslie and three others went into partnership. All of them were businessmen, and Ainslie was manager, so the factory was now under the personal supervision of one of the proprietors. Ainslie realised that Leith was pre-eminent as the port of entry for wine in Scotland, and shrewdly decided to specialise in bottlemaking. The business got established in a modest way, and despite continuing bitter rivalry from Newcastle, the Leith Glass Company survived.

After more than forty years at the Citadel works, Ainslie sold the business to James Balfour of Pilrig in 1728. Balfour was an entrepreneur, besides being laird of Pilrig. He had investments in several lines of business, and soon sold the Glasshouse to James Nimmo, who in turn sold it to Robert Wightman. In 1750 John Syme bought the site from Wightman. Syme was a carpenter and shipbuilder. He cleared the glasshouse site and set up a shipyard there. But what Syme bought and cleared was only the burnt-out remains of the glasshouse, for a disastrous fire in 1747 had brought glassmaking there to an end.

The fire decided Wightman and his partners to remove to South Leith, where the Sands offered plenty of room for development. The Town Council granted a feu, and the first glasshouse on the Sands was built by soldiers stationed at Edinburgh Castle. This was because in the aftermath of the '45 Rebellion skilled workmen were scarce, and bricklayers could not be found. The firm was now officially the Edinburgh Glasshouse Co., but in Leith it was known as the Bottle-house Company, for bottles had remained the specialty, and Leith bottles were becoming well known.

In response to growing demand a second 'cone' was erected on the Sands and began production in 1764. Green glass bottles, mainly for wine, had hitherto been the sole support of the business, but with growing confidence production was expanded into the manufacture of white glass bottles for chemists and others. By 1783 there was a third 'cone' at work, making flint glass, and seven years later crown window glass was coming from a fourth kiln. Leith was now growing fast and business was diversifying. A second firm, the Leith Glasshouse Company, was set up in 1790, and soon the two companies were operating seven furnaces between them. This level of production continued for the next twenty-five years.

Between 400 and 500 men were then employed in the glassworks, and the skilled workers in the industry were the highest wage-earners in Leith, taking home 21s to 30s weekly. Apart from the firms already mentioned, James Ranken was also in business from 1773 manufacturing crystal. His son Francis succeeded him in 1798, specialising in crystal drops and candlesticks. The famous chandeliers in the Edinburgh Assembly Rooms were designed and executed by Francis Ranken.

The melancholy fact is that this prosperous glass industry at Leith was destroyed by punitive taxation. First imposed in 1695, the duty on glass was withdrawn three years later, but reimposed in 1745. The duty was then 3s 4d per cwt for ordinary bottles, but this rate was repeatedly increased until it afforded a prime example of the law of diminishing returns. By 1822 the duty had reached the fantastic level of 98s per cwt, but by then the Edinburgh Glasshouse Co. had gone out of business. Their four kilns were advertised for sale in 1815. The Leith Glasshouse Co. kept going with two kilns. The Government belatedly reduced the tax on glass in 1825, but it was too late. The two remaining 'cones' were soon cold.

Soap-boiling was another early enterprise in Leith. A business naturally linked with the sea, since it used whale oil and fish offal, its origin in the port can be traced to a report made to the Privy Council in 1619 on foreign soap:

> with which this Kingdom is maist shamefully and misdecentlie abused, the samyn being composed of such pestiferous and filthie ingredients as no civil Kingdom, yea the very rude barbarians will nocht allow nor permit the lyke to be sold amongis thame, and in the country quhair it is made thair is no person of any condition quhatsomever, maisteris nor servandis, that will make use of it.

Nicolas Udwart, son of the Provost of Edinburgh, began making soap in Leith. His patent lapsed in 1640, but whether or not he was still in business then does not appear. The 1640s and 1650s were difficult times for business in Leith. Civil war, with urgent recruiting for the covenanting army, plague in 1645 carrying off almost two-thirds of the population, followed by the Cromwellian occupation, must have made all business hazardous. Nevertheless in 1649 James Riddell got permission to erect a soapwork in the Dubraw (St. Andrew Street), and there 'at the Sign of the Anchor' Riddell's soapwork was famous for many years.

In the mid-seventeenth century, then, there were two soapworks in Leith. James Riddell was succeeded in the business by his son George, who continued till 1697, when he sold out to James Balfour of Pilrig. The Riddell family were well-known, and Riddell's Close (later Market Street) perpetuated their name. The other soapwork stood at the head of the Rotten Row (Water Street) and was known as 'the old Soap-house of Leith'. This building, presumably the place where Udwart had begun soap-boiling, passed to a succession of proprietors until Robert Douglas acquired it. Like James Balfour, Douglas had a finger in many pies. His early days as a soap-boiler in Leith were enlivened by the town council of Edinburgh warning him that he must not live in Leith under a penalty of 500 merks. This was Edinburgh asserting her authority as proprietor of Leith. Anyone practising a trade or running a business in Leith must become a burgess of Edinburgh, and must live within the royalty of the city. Whether Mr Douglas conformed or not is not known, but he certainly remained in business.

In the course of the eighteenth century soapmaking became a staple industry in Leith, although never a large employer of labour. After the middle of the century the growing town provided favourable conditions for expansion. The firm of Jamison and Paton began business in 1782 and soon became one of the largest firms of its kind in Britain, with a factory in London opened in 1789. In Leith they overshadowed the smaller concern of Anderson and Cundell, who employed only seven or eight men, compared with the forty to fifty labourers working with Jamison and Paton. This firm moved in 1800 to Sheriff Brae, where, as Jamison and Auld, they continued for many years.

Robert Douglas did not confine himself to making soap. He began refining sugar in Leith in 1677. He was also involved with pottery and starch-making, but soap and sugar remained his prime interests. The sugar-house stood next to the soapwork in the Rotten Row, and here were produced loaf and powdered sugar, candy, molasses and rum. The Sugar Company partnership broke up in 1725, probably on the death of Robert Douglas, who by then had been almost half a century in the business. Sugar refining then had a precarious existence until 1757, when another sugarhouse was erected in the Kirkgate and operated by Alexander Innes and Partners. They lasted only five years; then after standing empty for four years the refinery started up again with a group of Englishmen in charge. They also failed, as did Thomas and William Parker, who succeeded them in 1770. Finally Anderson & Cundell moved in — the same firm who also had the smaller of the two soapworks.

Towards the end of the century prospects for sugar refining seemed brighter, and other firms made their entry. The Leith Sugar Refining Co. had premises in Coburg Street, and in 1804 William Macfie & Co. began operations in Elbe Street. The Macfies were prominent in the port, and in the mid-nineteenth century one of the family served for some years as Member of Parliament for the Leith District of Burghs.

Other businesses had their day in the town. None of them were

Cooper: Servicing a cask — a craft as old as the wine trade in Leith.

large employers, but there are points of interest about each. Pinmaking began about 1663 and continued for over a century. Cotton and linen weaving was carried on at Bonnington Mills, and Robert Douglas tried to start a pottery, but failed, it was said, for lack of capital. A few years later William Montgomerie of Machrie Hill, with a partner, is said to have erected a 'Potthouse' in 1703 for the production of 'Laim, purselane, earthenware', but there is no evidence that porcelain was ever produced at Leith. Later in the eighteenth century John and David Stead had a flourishing wool-card factory off Leith Walk on a site commemorated by the name of Stead's Place. Cardmaking began in the 1660s, but the early years were disastrous and a great deal of money was lost. The Union of 1707, abolishing customs duty between Scotland and England, greatly benefited cardmaking. Before then the smuggling of cheap secondhand cards from England had been a major obstacle to the development of the business in Leith.

Brickmaking, distilling and tanning were all carried on in a small way, and one interesting development was dyeing. War with Spain had stopped trade with the Canary and Cape Verde islands, where a lichen was obtained for the manufacture of archel, used to make a blue dye. Prizes were offered for a viable substitute, and Cuthbert Gordon of Leith was soon making a dye he claimed was better than archel. He and his brothers opened a factory in the Kirkgate where he set up business, using a lichen found in the West Highlands. Gordon called his dye cudbear — derived from his own Christian name — and cudbear, combined with various other substances, produced a range of colours. The Kirkgate premises went on fire in January 1773, and Cuthbert and George Gordon opened a new factory near the foot of the Walk; but like so many other promising ventures in Leith at that period, the firm lacked capital, and three years later the Gordons were bankrupt and the cudbear patent was bought by George Mackintosh of Glasgow, who removed the manufacture to that city in 1777.

Trading through Leith increased steadily through the nineteenth century, and a mainstay of the export trade was coal from the Lothian pits. In 1838 the first railway line was brought to Leith Docks as a branch from the Edinburgh and Dalkeith Railway. At first the wagons were horse-drawn, and it was only after the line was taken over by the North British Railway that locomotive power was introduced in 1849. The coalfields were also large importers of pit-props, and the timber trade was increasingly important to Leith — both soft and hardwoods from the Baltic and Canada. Grain also from Canada and Australia became another mainstay of the import trade.

The improvement of communications by road, rail and sea benefited Leith, which was well placed to develop as a main distributing centre. From the early years of the nineteenth century William Thorburn of Leith was one of the biggest importers of tea in the country, and his premises in the Kirkgate were patronised by a widespread clientèle of discriminating tea-drinkers. Thorburn, with some younger contemporaries, including Andrew Melrose who had begun business in Leith in 1812, successfully challenged the long-standing monopoly of the East India Company in tea-trading. Melrose is credited with placing the first 'free trade' order for 600 packages of tea with Jardine Matheson in Canton in November 1833.

In the late twentieth century it is difficult to realise the immense amount of physical labour that was involved in the trading of the port of Leith. With very little mechanical aid, thousands of hands had to be employed. The First World War changed the industrial scene permanently. The post-war recession in Leith extended to the outbreak of the Second World War, but the technical advances in that same period meant that the amount of work done in Leith pre-1914 could now be done by a much smaller workforce. One consequence of this was a great increase in emigration, which continued after 1945. Only in very recent years has there been a realisation that no return to the old work-pattern is even desirable. Leith's industrial future will not depend on a few large employers, but on a diversity of smaller businesses engaging in many types of work, giving steady employment for twelve months in the year.

CHAPTER 4

The Links

From the beginning the Links have been integral to Leith. The original settlement at the mouth of the river was built on the Links, and today, after all the changes and vicissitudes of the centuries, the Shore and the Links remain, and alone remain, from the earliest days of the port. Both have changed greatly, but they cannot be removed, and the Links have been the setting for much local history.

Centuries ago this area was the 'coney warren', and the name evokes a picture of rough sand dunes affording rabbits for the pot, but by the eighteenth century the last rabbit had been snared and the old name lost its significance. This was common land extensively covered with rough grass and whin, which in wet weather became spongy, for it was undrained.

Apart from the rather poor grazing to be had there, the Links, much more extensive than today, had two main uses — for recreation and for military purposes. In those unsettled times all men were obliged to carry arms, and periodically these were inspected, and instruction was given in their use. Weaponshowings were organised on Logan's Lea, and in 1602 John Logan, the laird in charge of the parade, was in trouble with the Town Council. Edinburgh had sent Bailie Alex. Pearson as inspecting officer, but the ensign-bearers had not accorded the visiting bailie any of the usual courtesies. He was mortified and complained to the Town Council, who issued an order that in future all the ensigns at Leith weaponshowings would be borne by nominees of the city — an early example of the bad feeling between city and port.

It was on the Links that the English army deployed in the spring of 1560, besieging Leith. Here they dug trenches, tried to undermine the town wall, and threw up three gun emplacements for the besieging cannon. Of these three mounds, originally named after the captains of the gun crews, Mount Somerset, Mount Pelham and Mount Falcon, the first acquired the title of Giant's Brae, the second became Lady Fyfe's Brae, recalling the Countess of Fife, who owned Hermitage House in the eighteenth century, situated behind the present East Hermitage Place, and the third, Mount Falcon, was

Leith Races: Scene in the 1850s on the Sands. Notice the glassworks 'cones', the Signal Tower and the Martello Tower.

removed when Bowling Green Street was built (now part of a new housing complex off Great Junction Street).

The Covenanting army under General Leslie was encamped on the Links and mustered there before the ill-judged march to defeat at the Battle of Dunbar in 1650. But from an even earlier period the Links were the scene of archery contests. Hugo Arnot, the historian of Edinburgh, and himself a Leith man, claims that a silver arrow given by the town of Musselburgh was shot for as early as 1603. The Company of Archers was a club or society of Scottish noblemen intent on preserving the skills of archery. As the Society's records were destroyed by fire in the early eighteenth century, nothing is known of its foundation, and little of its early activities. The association of the Archers with Leith Links, however, is vouched for by a minute of Edinburgh town council on 1st November 1665, when the treasurer was appointed to provide a silver arrow to the value of fifty shillings sterling 'to be shott for in the Lynks...' King Charles II approved of the Society of Archers, and in 1676 the Privy Council confirmed a set of Regulations and donated £20 sterling to purchase a prize for competition. In 1709 Edinburgh town council presented the Company with a silver arrow for annual competition, and four years later the society was erected into an incorporation with the title 'The Royal Company of Archers'. Several more regulations to govern the competition for the silver arrow were introduced by the Town

51

Council in 1726, and it was then laid down that the contest should take place on the Links of Leith each year on the second Monday of July at 10 a.m. 'if good weather'. If the weather was unsuitable, the event would be postponed until the first fair Monday following. Notice of the competition was to be given on the last Monday of June and the first Monday of July 'by beat of drum throughout Edinburgh'.

These regulations were approved before the first parade of the Archers subsequent to the '15 Rebellion. The intriguing fact about these noblemen and gentlemen of Scotland is that they were almost all Jacobites — and known to be such; yet it was under Queen Anne's government that they became an incorporation. Arnot's account is interesting:

> The first time that in consequence of their charter, they displayed any military parade, was in A.D. 1714... They did not hesitate to ingross in their minute-book, in terms which could not be misunderstood, that they remembered, on his birthday, the health of an exiled Prince. And on the 14th June, the Earl of. Cromarty, their captain-general, altho then upwards of 80 years of age, and the Earl of Wemyss, as their lieutenant-general, marched at the head of above fifty noblemen and gentlemen, cloathed in uniform, equipped in military array, and distinguished by their proper standards, from the parliament-square to the palace of Holyrood-house, thence to Leith, where they shot for the silver arrow given by the city of Edinburgh; and returned in similar parade; having received from the different guards which they passed, the same honours that are paid to any body of the King's forces...

The next year, Cromarty having died, the Earl of Wemyss headed the procession, which numbered more than twice the turnout of the previous year.

After 1743 the Archers went, as it were, underground. They were widely suspected as being a disaffected body, and the '45 Rebellion forced them to be very circumspect. It was said that the Government set spies to watch their activities, and only in the 1770s, led by the highly respected William St. Clair of Roslin, did the Archers revive and become the honoured and honourable body they have since remained.

There is no possibility of knowing when, where or how the game of golf started. No doubt the ability to strike a ball from a distance into a small hole could have been a matter of challenge and competition from very ancient times. As early as 1616 John Moir, a Leith man,

Return from the Races: Constitution Road in the 18th century.

was fined £50 by the Edinburgh magistrates for kicking Sir Alexander Hay and striking him with a golf club. The early game was informal, and the rules were simply agreed between opponents at the start of each game. Golf appealed to all classes, for the equipment was simple, the Links were common ground, and skill was unhampered by social distinctions. Well-known anecdotes of the game at Leith tell of how in 1640 King Charles I heard of rebellion in Ireland while engaged in a game there, and of how 'Golfer's Land' in the Canongate was built with the winnings from a match in which the Duke of Albany was partnered by John Paterson, a poor shoemaker, against two Englishmen. That story is probably apocryphal, but Golfer's Land was the property of a Leith maltman, Nicol Paterson, in 1632, and later of his son John, both of whom were ardent golfers.

Passing from vague traditions of the game in early times, it is a fact that a group of well-to-do Edinburgh addicts, in the manner of the times, formed themselves into a club. Eighteenth-century Edinburgh housed many clubs, some with arcane rules and shibboleths. The Leith golf club at first had no special name. They called themselves 'The Gentlemen Golfers' and met on Leith Links every Saturday — 'play day' as they called it. After a day's golf they gathered in the evening at a tavern in the Kirkgate, to dine together, settle their bets, and make and accept challenges to play the next Saturday.

Like the game itself, this club had no formal foundation date, but after some years the idea of a trophy for competition was born. No doubt they were aware of the Archers' silver arrow, but perhaps a stronger motive was the desire for some kind of official recognition. The Links were common ground, so the golfers had no exclusive rights there. The Incorporation of Carters in Leith had since 1663 paid an annual rent for grazing horses on the Links, and black cattle were also grazed there by various owners. It cannot be supposed that flying golf balls were welcomed by carters and graziers, so the application by the golfers in 1744 for a trophy could well have been intended to strengthen their position as users of the Links.

The magistrates were sympathetic, and proposed presenting a silver golf club for annual competition. The one condition attached was that there should be specific rules agreed for this competition. The golfers gratefully agreed, drew up thirteen Rules which they called 'Articles and Laws in Playing at Golf' and submitted them for approval. These were the first acknowledged Rules of Golf, and when, ten years later, the Gentlemen of Fife invited the 'Gentlemen Golfers of Leith' to join them in forming a golf club at St. Andrews, these thirteen rules were taken and adapted to local conditions. The 13th Rule in particular had special local significance in Leith:

> Neither Trench, Ditch or Dyke, made for the preservation of the Links, nor the Scholar's Holes or the Soldier's Lines, Shall be accounted a Hazard, But the Ball is to be taken out Teed and play'd with any Iron Club.

Troops were regularly quartered in Leith. Officers were billeted with reluctant private households, and the men occupied a permanent encampment on the Links. This was 'the Soldier's Lines', and the nuisance continued until the erection of Leith Fort in 1780. 'The Scholar's Holes' referred to the ground adjacent to the town wall at the churchyard. The Grammar School met in the King James Hospital at the south-west corner of the churchyard, so here a series of short holes was laid out (in modern terms a pitch-and-putt course) for the benefit of boys learning the game, and for old men no longer fit for the main course.

There is no doubt the course on the Links was a bad one. It consisted of five holes, and the layout bore little resemblance to a modern course, apart from the length of the holes. Fairways were strips of better herbage which was naturally more closely grazed than the whin-covered dunes. Even the vicinity of the holes received no special attention, and horse droppings and cow-pats were accepted as hazards, like the many pools. Horsemen and pedestrians used the

Feathers for a Golf Ball: The 'Feathery Ball' was in use until the 1840s, when it was succeeded by the 'Guttie'. A hatful of feathers was needed for one ball.

Links constantly, and these presented further hazards to the golfers. Throughout the eighteenth century the Honourable Company of Edinburgh Golfers on Leith Links, as they eventually came to be called, spent much thought and money in attempts to improve the course, and they succeeded up to a point, but it was an unending struggle.

More time and money were spent on drainage than on any other scheme. The land is so flat that even in the twentieth century draining on the Links presents problems. An open drainage system was adopted, with a pattern of ditches which tended to become waterlogged. The Honourable Company also constructed a roadway over the Links in an effort to persuade the public to cross the golf course at that point rather than just where their fancy directed. Today that road, from the foot of Restalrig Road to Links Gardens, is a great convenience, but when it was first provided it was largely ignored.

The golfers were enthusiastic; they believed in their club's future,

C

and built themselves a Golf-house. They had originally met in Luckie Clephane's tavern near the foot of Easter Road. Later a move was made to Mrs Straiton's, which was a popular howff. But the golfers wanted more privacy, and some kind of changing-room where they could store their gear and enjoy adequate dining facilities. The Golf-house, on the site of the present Leith Academy Secondary School, was rented to an innkeeper who ran it as a tavern. Some years later a bowling-green was constructed to the rear of the Golf-house. Two rooms in the house were reserved for club members, where they dined and stored clubs and uniforms.

The uniform was important. Under a strict rule no member was allowed to play until properly dressed. The distinctive garb at once identified members of the Honourable Company, who now had almost a preemptive right to play on the course in consideration of all they had done to improve it. The Links were none the less common land, and anyone could play golf there. William St. Clair was Captain of the Company in 1771, and his portrait, hanging in the Hall of the Royal Company of Archers, shows him in a red jacket and waistcoat, with a blue Kilmarnock bonnet. This is the earliest recorded example of the golfers' uniform, but it was changed several times. In 1790 John Paterson, the club tailor, was ordered to provide the waiter in the Golf-house with a uniform consisting of 'a scarlet plush Coat with a blue velvet Cope and a Bluff Waistcoat and Breeches of Cloth'. Presumably 'Cope' is a cap.

In an age when heavy drinking and gambling were taken as a matter of course, Saturday night in the Golf-house was a convivial occasion. Many odd challenges and wagers were made. A good player might offer an opponent a stroke a hole, but a more intriguing challenge was the offer to play the whole match with one ball. Balls were of leather stuffed with feathers; they were remarkably light and hard, and a good player might drive 180 to 200 yards. The point of the challenge, however, was that the course was wet, with many puddles and wet ditches, and once the ball was soaked it was near useless. Iron clubs were also hard on the ball, straining the leather stitching. The rules stipulated that the same ball must be played between the teeing ground and the hole, but it was permissible to use a fresh ball for each hole played. In an average match several balls would normally be used. Another favourite challenge was to play only with the iron clubs — 'Irons all' as it was called — but this was eventually forbidden as it did too much damage to the very restricted

Leith Links 1829: Looking towards John's Place. Golf was not the only activity on the Links. The grass was valued as a bleaching green.

areas of smooth turf. A long-remembered match took place in 1798 between Alex Wood, in his 70th year, and his grandson in his seventh year, against Dr Duncan, in his 50th year, and his son in his fifth year. The Woods won, and the challenge was renewed and the match repeated the next year. This became an annual match for almost twenty years, and the Woods always won — narrowly but convincingly. Seven strokes a hole was reckoned good average play over Leith Links, and championships were won on an average of $6\frac{1}{2}$ strokes a hole. Much better scores were being returned at St. Andrews, but the Fife course was drier and easier than that at Leith.

In the late eighteenth century large villas in their own grounds began to appear on the fringes of the Links — Pirniefield House, Prospect Bank House, Hermitage House and others. This was tolerable, but the owners of these villas grazed cows and horses on the Links, and were willing to pay for grazing rights. The golfers were not pleased, and in 1787 they got a 19-year lease of the Links for £37.14.6 per annum, and continued to spend money on improvements. They had a new set of drains constructed, but this work had hardly been completed when the place was overrun by 'the Mid Lothian Volunteers and other Cavalry' who drilled and manoeuvred, and pranced and galloped all over the golf course, doing extensive damage. Protests were useless. There was a war on, and civilian inconvenience was of no consequence. A second 19-year lease was taken in 1806, but the Honourable Company were not now an important tenant. Indeed when the second lease was taken, they were three years behind with the rent. Hard times now brought a change of attitude to grazing, and they tried to rent the grass to bring in some money, but without success. Prospective tenants alleged that the grazing had deteriorated and was now worthless.

With the ending of the Napoleonic War the Town Council became much more interested in feuing ground bordering the Links for building high-class residential accommodation, and were no longer concerned about the complaints of the golfers. From the beginning of the nineteenth century the Honourable Company were in trouble, for an increasing number of members were forsaking Leith in favour of Musselburgh — a drier course, although it was five miles further along the coast. As a result the golfers at Leith were always behind with the rent. In 1815 the Thistle Golf Club was founded, and for some time occupied a lean-to shed attached to the Golf-house. This collapsed in a storm in 1822, but the Thistle Club refused to share the Golf-house with the Honourable Company.

The Edinburgh golfers seem to have had little understanding of their plight, for they continued to spend money on improving the Golf-house, but it became necessary to take out a mortgage on the property in 1824. £500 raised in this way was absorbed in paying outstanding debts, and a second mortgage raised £200 which went in the same way. The end came in August 1833 when the contents of the Golf-house were rouped by order of the Sheriff. The following year the Golf-house itself was sold for £1130, thus ending the connection of the Honourable Company of Edinburgh Golfers with Leith. For the rest of the nineteenth century they played at Musselburgh, before moving to their present ground at Muirfield.

The history of the Links must include Leith Sands. Before the era of land reclamation, before the advent of docks and industrial plant so greatly altered the scene, the Links and Sands could be seen as one, for the tussocky grass gave way to smooth sand on a level beach. The very slight incline towards the sea meant that at low tide a considerable extent of sand was exposed. Like the Links, the Sands were a popular recreation ground from early times. The wide sweep of firm sand between high and low watermarks was long popular for exercising horses, and horse-racing had been an established sport long before the King and the City of Edinburgh gave official approval

Golf Tournament: Some of the competitors in the last professional tournament on the Links, 17th May 1867. L to R, A. Strath, D. Park, Bob Kirk, James Anderson, Jamie Dunn, William Dow, Willie Dunn, A. Greig, Tom Morris, Tom Morris jun. and George Morris.

to Leith Races. Two silver cups were given as prizes in 1665, and so began the annual carnival and saturnalia which came to be both loved and hated in Leith.

At first, and for many years, the races were held at irregular intervals and at different times in the year. From the mid-eighteenth century the event was established in the summer, and what had been originally a day's racing expanded to two days and then to a week, with more and more prizes at stake. The golf course may have been poor by modern standards, but even by the standards of the eighteenth century the Sands were unsuitable for racing. Hugo Arnot, who was familiar with the course, remarked that the Sands were 'heavy and fatiguing for the horses, especially if they are not of strong bottom'. Yet Leith Races attracted entries from a very wide area, many coming from the northern counties of England.

The race course stretched originally from near the foot of the present Constitution Street, to Seafield. One circuit, to Seafield and back, measured two miles, and a heat consisted of two circuits. The first rules of racing on Leith Sands bore no resemblance to the Jockey Club rules of the twentieth century: Most races at Leith were run for the best of three heats, which meant that the ultimate winner would have to run twelve miles on very heavy going. The starting-post was also the finishing-post, and 200 yards from it the distance-post was driven into the sand. At the end of a heat, as the first horse passed the finishing-post, a flag was dropped, and all those horses not yet past the distance-post were eliminated.

There were many strange and complicated rules, and perhaps the oddest circumstance of all was that the rules were made by the Town Council, who changed them as they thought fit. Management of the Races was in the hands of the Company of Scots Hunters, whose secretary acted as treasurer to the Races. The original King's Cup of 1665 was changed around 1720 to a Gold Plate, and other cups and plates were added to the prize list from time to time; but in the later eighteenth century these trophies were converted into purses, and Subscription Races became popular. This was the eighteenth-century form of sponsorship.

As the century advanced, Leith Races came down in the world. In mid-century Robert Fergusson celebrated the annual event in rollicking verse, but had he lived to the end of the century he would have found the Races disreputable even by comparison with the raffish circus he had known. Race week came to be dreaded in Leith for the drunkenness, fighting and vandalism that had become inevitably associated with the event. In 1816 the Races were moved to Musselburgh — not to relieve the people of Leith, but to find a better racecourse. The Sands had finally been recognised as unsuitable. Edinburgh town council had had a Plan and Estimate prepared with a view to constructing a racecourse on the Meadows, but that came to nothing, and the Musselburgh course — flat, dry turf — was a great improvement on Leith Sands.

Twenty years later horse-racing on the Sands was revived. This was not the old event returning from Musselburgh, but a new venture — 'Leith Annual Subscription Races'. Public opinion in the port was outraged. Churches and other bodies protested and memorialised the Town Council without success, but there was a groundswell of opposition which could not be ignored, although the magistrates took no action. It was the Dock Commission which eventually dealt with matters, prohibiting the erection of booths or tents on the Sands during the Races. That was in 1856. The race promoters held on for some years, but the last meeting took place on 22nd September 1859, and no regrets were ever expressed.

Racing occupied one week, but the Sands were by no means

The End Game: Golf was prohibited on Leith Links after the Craigentinny ground was acquired by the Town Council in 1907. This picture shows what must have been one of the last games on the Links.

deserted for the rest of the year. Sea-bathing came into vogue in the eighteenth century, with medical approval. By the end of the century salt water was regarded as a sovereign cure for all kinds of ailments, and Leith bade fair to become a convenient, desirable resort. A bathing machine was set up on the Sands in 1750 but it did not survive for long. It was a stationary contraption standing below high watermark, holding four people. There was no question of swimming; bathers undressed, bathed and dressed again all inside the box, which had no floor. An attendant was required to carry prospective bathers through the shallow water to the machine, and this venture ended when no attendant could be found. Ten years later a better type of bathing-machine was introduced. This one was mounted on wheels, and soon there were several of these on the Sands near the Glass-house.

Edinburgh folk who could afford it liked taking houses for the summer near the coast or in the country. This market now boomed, and accommodation was advertised as bathing quarters, all along the coast from Granton to Portobello. At the same time, however, glassmaking was expanding, and the addition of other kilns to the original one was a significant development — the beginning of the industrialisation of the coastline. A final effort to make sea-bathing pay at Leith was the erection of Seafield Baths in 1813. Here there was no swimming, but the building accommodated seventeen hot, cold and tepid baths, and a large plunge bath. Hotel accommodation was also provided for those who wished to take a course of bathing. But this did nothing to stop the ruination of the seashore, and Portobello soon took over as the prime resort for the citizens of the capital.

While bathing failed at Leith, swimming began to flourish. By the middle of last century the Forth Swimming Club was very active in the summer. The club favoured the Chain Pier at Trinity for organised events, and swimmers had to contend with the vagaries of wind, currents and temperature, for indoor swimming baths were unknown. Amid a variety of events the two main contests were for 'fast swimming' — a 300-yard race — and 'long diving', which was, in fact, swimming under water. This sport remained popular all through the century until the first indoor pool — the Victoria Baths — was opened in 1896.

The Links were increasingly used for sports and games, and grazing animals were now seen as a nuisance. In 1839 there was trouble with boys chasing horses at grass. About thirty animals were seen galloping in all directions — a public danger. From then on only sheep and cows were allowed to graze. But on an October day in 1862 a lady was attacked by a cow on the Links, and was butted and trampled. Two golfers came to her aid, and one broke his club over the cow. It was becoming obvious that grazing must be stopped.

Golf on the Links still flourished. The Thistle Club had to share the course with the Seafield and the Leith Golf clubs, but most players belonged to no club; they simply played among themselves to their own satisfaction. Then in 1840 the Leith Games were instituted with permission from the magistrates. Almost certainly they were intended as a counterblast to the objectionable horse races. The two events were held within a fortnight of each other, and by request of the Games Committee the sale of intoxicating drink was forbidden at the Games. A modern spectator would have found the Games intolerably boring, for each event took a very long time to organise and start. But great crowds attended, and a stand for 500 spectators was erected for the occasion. As well as athletics there was a quoiting competition,

Highland dancing, wrestling, vaulting, climbing the greasy pole in pursuit of a ham, and shooting competitions on the Sands. But the Games were merely part of a great Fair. There were gaming tables (illegal, but still operating), conjurors, acrobats, lollipop women, ballad-singers, barrows of fruit and cakes, and cheap-jacks selling 'genuine' jewellery.

Leith Games became a great institution which came to an end, oddly enough, through the improvement of the Links. When the rough grass and hummocky ground were smoothed and tidied, and trees and trim paths and mown grass replaced the old common, the Magistrates asked the Games Committee to become responsible for making good any damage done during the Games. The Committee divided over this, and for two years rival Games were held on the same day, on the Links and at Powderhall, where they came under new management.

The Dock Porters were traditionally attached to the game of quoits, which they played on ground on the West Links. Towards the end of the eighteenth century the quoiting ground became deserted — which may have been a side-effect of the war with France, when every able-bodied man was either hard at work or pressed into the armed forces. In 1839, however, the *Scotsman* reported a revival of the game, and this continued through the rest of the century, fostered especially by the St. James' Quoiting Club, which in 1895 was given a new ground on the north side near Seafield.

Edinburgh's long possession of the Links came to an end in 1856, when Leith town council bought the ground. Almost at once a stream of petitions came before the Council seeking facilities on the Links for various games. Two cricket pitches were laid and two bowling greens constructed opposite Links Place, but it was many years before any effort was made to improve the ground overall. The Great Leith Improvement Scheme in the 1880s marked the real transformation of the Links. Work was then put in hand to level the ground and mark off the traditional paths, which were top-dressed with ashes from the gasworks; and, on the suggestion of the Rev. Dr James Mitchell of South Leith parish church, trees were planted — not by the Town Council, but by the residents in the villas surrounding the Links; and Mr Munro Ferguson, M.P. for Leith Burghs, provided one hundred trees from his estate. The Town Council contributed shrubs, had the grass cut, and erected railings everywhere to protect this new amenity.

The conversion of the Links made a great impression locally, and with cricketers, golfers and footballers all clamouring for space and facilities, the Council applied to the 'Scotch Secretary', a recent Government appointment, for a Provisional Order to enable them to make bye-laws for the Links. No fewer than eleven cricket clubs were soon sharing the East Links.

Football was not universally welcomed. Two Leithers raised an action of Declarator to have the playing of football on the Links stopped. They claimed that the pursuit of this pastime had had the effect of bringing the Links into a condition of 'sandy desert' varied by 'successions of mudholes', and that the locality was a scene of hideous uproar, rendering the Links unfit to be used by respectable persons. The action failed, but there was much popular prejudice against the game, which quickly wore through the thin grass cover. Football was confined to the area in front of the High School and confined to the six winter months between 15th September and 15th March. At any other time the game could only be played by special permission.

Golf had become a public nuisance and was forbidden from June to September, and even in winter it was banned between 12 noon and 2 p.m. It was unthinkable that Leithers should be deprived of golfing facilities, and the dilemma was solved by the Town Council leasing ground at Craigentinny in 1907, where a nine-hole course was made under the direction of Ben Sayers. This course, later extended to eighteen holes, was just outside the Leith boundary, but its acquisition meant the virtual end of golf on Leith Links.

In 1889 a proposal was made to have an artificial pond on the Links, mainly for the benefit of model yacht enthusiasts. Nothing was done then, but after the turn of the century a pool was constructed, which stood for some years, until between the wars it fell into disuse. The final touch of splendour in the metamorphosis of the Links was the erection of a bandstand, music being dispensed there on Saturday afternoons for the delectation of the 'respectable' part of the community. This attraction also faded after the Second World War; and 1939 also saw the removal of the Victorian railings which had enclosed much of the grass. By general consent this has greatly improved the appearance of the Links, which remain the port's main recreation area.

CHAPTER 5

Health and Housing

Life in mediaeval Leith was maintained at a basic level. Much of what is thought necessary today did not then exist. The poor, who formed the great majority of the population, had no flooring in their homes, and very little furniture. Some who were better off had timber-built houses and a modicum of comfort, but even so, in modern eyes, conditions were primitive.

This undistinguished beginning was improved upon in the fifteenth century, when the port's enhanced status as a burgh of barony, and the establishment of trade incorporations, attracted more business to the village. The beginning of building at the King's Wark gave local employment. The canons of St. Anthony, cultivating a large garden and orchard, demonstrated the possibilities of that fertile ground. The same period also saw the rise of notable families of sea adventurers — shipmasters who were also shipowners and traders — and pirates too, when opportunity occurred. Many of the merchant skippers of the fifteenth century bore names still common in Leith — Dawson, Forster, Robertson, Blyth, Anderson, Paterson, Hay and Pennycook — and some like the Bartons and Falconers not only made names for themselves but tidy fortunes. When the Earl of Hertford descended on Leith in 1544, this was already the chief port in Scotland, and its vicinity was favoured by prosperous Edinburgh citizens for second homes. These outsiders avoided the 'closets' of the original Leith as a dangerous area of infection.

Plague was a frequent problem in Leith, always open to infection from incoming cargoes and crews, and perhaps the place was never entirely free of that scourge, although the extent of the trouble varied from year to year. Throughout the fifteenth and sixteenth centuries several severe outbreaks were recorded. The burning of Leith in 1544 and 1547 would at least destroy persistent pockets of infection, and after the siege of 1560 the old 'closets' were not rebuilt. The new village that was then developed was arranged in streets and wynds instead of the earlier disorganised jumble of buildings. That year 1560 also marked the suppression of the old religion. The Preceptory of St. Anthony was no longer officially recognised, and along the

The Day Nursery: 28 Tolbooth Wynd, 'for the care of children whose mothers are obliged to work out'. In 1909 the daily fee for one child was 3d, and for two, three and four children of one family, 5d, 7d & 9d. Open daily except Sundays from 5.30 a.m. to 6.30 p.m.

boundary wall of its garden a line of breweries gradually developed. That was the beginning of the Yeardheids, and this line of development was dictated by the fact that the Greenside Burn flowed in that direction towards the Water of Leith, and each brewery drew its water from that source. For the next two centuries this area was considered to be outside Leith proper, and documents referring to the district invariably describe it as 'Leith, Yardheads and the Territory of St. Anthony's'. In that same period there was very little increase in population, the total remaining at around 4500 inhabitants.

The last visitation of bubonic plague in Leith occurred in 1645, and this was by far the most serious outbreak ever experienced in the port. More than half the people died in the summer and autumn of that year and, with the population reduced to not much more than 2000, it was near the end of the century before the deficit was made up again. In this connection the annals of Leith include one volume of unique interest, for the kirk session of the parish church were then expected to assume the burden of local government, and the session clerk, David Aldinstone, left a remarkable account of all that was done for public health and safety during the months of plague. The elders met frequently — sometimes daily — and while there is a gap

The Kitchen in the House of Call: Model lodginghouse established in 1872 at 3 Parliament Street.

of some weeks, during which Aldinstone himself was probably ill, the clerk yet recorded a detailed account of the situation in Leith throughout that year of suffering, fear and near despair.

Infection was first confirmed among the old women in the King James Hospital, but soon it was raging through the village. The time was late spring, following a winter of scarcity after a bad harvest in 1644. In their weakened condition people fell easy victims to the disease, but there was no panic. For some weeks the plague was accepted with a shrug as a frequent, though unwelcome, visitor. Long experience had taught people the basic remedies. The need for cleanliness was well understood, and measures were put in hand to redd the streets, fumigate infected premises and boil all clothing. Where a case of infection was confirmed, the sufferer and all the family were confined to the house to prevent the spread of infection. It was as the summer advanced and the plague continued to increase with alarming speed that indifference turned to apprehension. A whole village of wooden shacks was set up on the East Links near Seafield, and all infected families were sent to live there while their own houses were fumigated.

The number of dead grew to the extent that burying them became a problem. The churchyard was not used: infected corpses were disposed of outside the village. At first the site of the old bastion at the

St. Ninian's Row: Now Church Street, North Leith. These old houses were demolished before 1914.

St. Anthony port was used, and later mass graves were dug in the West Links outside the wall. The early victims were provided with coffins, but this could not continue. Those who succumbed were simply wrapped in the sheet they died in and so were committed to the ground. Handling the dead was dangerous, and so many workmen and sledders died that it became difficult to find successors. The Links were denuded of whin, which was used for burning in infected houses, and the countryside was scoured as far afield as Kilsyth for fuel to keep the fumigating fires going. Huge cauldrons stood on the Links for boiling infected clothes, and a great stone kiln on Logan's Lea was reserved for those prepared to pay for their laundry being done separately from that of common folk. All this, of course, interfered with normal farming operations, so that there was no harvest, and another winter of scarcity and high prices faced the hapless Leithers. Those who could afford to left Leith for more salubrious quarters.

The virulence of infection began to diminish in the autumn, and at the beginning of November a tremendous rainstorm helped to wash away the last of the trouble. Leith greeted 1646 with relief, but long remembered the sufferings of the plague year. Yet the port always remained vulnerable to infection brought in from Europe. Also, while the principles of cleanliness and sanitation were recognised as ideals, the achievement of these ends remained a problem, so that even after the terrible experience of 1645 the village soon reverted to the state of things that had obtained before the plague, and there was no change until past the middle of the eighteenth century. By then the Industrial Revolution was transforming the village into a town, and several long-standing inconveniencies had become urgent problems requiring swift and drastic action.

The greatest of these troubles was the lack of an adequate water supply. In early times the Water of Leith, the Broughton Burn and the Greenside Burn provided sufficient water, but flowing through Edinburgh, both the Water of Leith and the Broughton Burn became heavily polluted from sewage and industrial effluent, and while the Yardheads breweries were served by the Greenside Burn, these wells were not available to the public. Larger houses also had wells sunk in their gardens, but these also were private. The few public wells were totally inadequate. Industries like sugar-refining and soap-boiling operated in Leith on a small scale, and under great difficulties, of which the greatest was the lack of any piped water. Without a better water supply there could never be any industrial expansion in Leith. As Leith was a possession of Edinburgh, it might be supposed that the city would have been concerned to provide adequate water in the port and so increase the value of her asset, but Edinburgh was not interested. However, in 1752 the Incorporation of Traffickers in Leith became aware that Edinburgh was intending to apply to Parliament for a renewal of the tax on ale. This was a levy of twopence on every pint of ale brewed in the city, and Leith-brewed ale was included. The Traffickers, with representatives from the other Leith corporations, asked the city to use some of the money from the ale tax to provide Leith with a supply of piped water, such as the city enjoyed. The magistrates said they could not make any promises until the Leithers produced a plan and estimate for the work.

This was an unexpectedly reasonable answer, and the Deacons of the corporations very quickly got estimates. There was no argument over the source of supply. Lochend loch was the obvious reservoir, and water would be brought to Leith through wooden pipes to a cistern in the town, from which pipes could be led to where water was needed. This work was to cost £600, and the Town Council agreed to

Sailors' Home: Opened 1885. A great institution, greatly appreciated in its day.

pay half of this sum if the other half was raised in Leith. Subscriptions were called for, and the work was immediately put in hand. A public appeal was launched by the incorporations, but this produced only £110. Edinburgh then contributed £150, and promised the rest of the money as soon as Leith kept its part of the bargain. On the other hand the local plumber who had been awarded the contract for the work had had no experience of an undertaking on this scale. He needed money at once to buy materials and pay wages, and there were no credit facilities. The work would have to be paid for as it progressed. In the end the incorporations had to find the rest of the money between them.

William Maitland was then writing his famous *History of Edinburgh,* and he added a chapter at the end of his book severely criticising the whole proposal. He maintained that Lochend loch was far too small for the purpose, that the water was unhygienic, and that the contractor was a fool, as he was laying the pipes fifteen feet below the ground, which would make repairs needlessly expensive, and that before long the whole scheme would have to be abandoned, a new source of water found, and much more expense incurred. All these criticisms were justified, but Maitland was not living in Leith, where

New Lane: Newhaven at the turn of the century was still an exclusive community with its own lifestyle.

there was a desperate sense of the need to get something done at once.

Within months it was plain that not nearly enough water was coming from Lochend, and the original pipes had to be replaced with others of a larger bore. The cistern, at the junction of Carpet Lane and Water Street, was also abandoned in favour of a much larger one at the foot of the Kirkgate, at the junction of Tolbooth Wynd and Water Street. Here the 'Big Pipes', as they were locally known, fed water in, and from this cistern piped water was led to industrial users, while the precious fluid was also available to the public by the bucketful. Apart from the Big Pipes there were then five public wells. The first was in the Kirkgate opposite the brickwork (later Brickwork Close); the second was in the south-west corner of the yard outside the Vaults in Giles Street; the third on the coalhill at Leith Brig; the fourth at the New Quay at the foot of Tolbooth Wynd; and the fifth at Bernard's Neuk in Bernard Street. The well at the New Quay was originally intended to serve ships in the harbour.

This was the state of the water supply when in 1771 an Act of Parliament was passed to have the streets of Leith, Yardheads and St. Anthony's cleansed and lighted and supplied with fresh water. The town was growing rapidly. From 1750 to 1800 the population rose from 5000 to over 16,000, and to accommodate the stream of country folk coming to Leith looking for work, a network of narrow wynds and lanes with two and three-storey tenements was hurriedly built. And there was no sanitation of any kind. Not only was there no piped water, there were no drains or sewers, no made roads — no causewaying or road bottoming — so that the wynds and closes were full of great potholes, deep in mud in winter, thick with dust in summer. Outside stairs further obstructed the thoroughfares, so that wheeled traffic passed through with difficulty and at great inconvenience to pedestrians. Many householders also kept pigs, geese or hens, which rooted and scratched among the piles of filth in the roadway. The last straw on this burden of misery was the lack of any public street lighting, so that after dark the wayfarer had to carry lantern or torch, or take a big chance and grope his way.

The Act of 1771 was a statement of intent. To make it effective provision was made for the election of thirty Police Commissioners. Policing, however, had nothing to do with crime. The Commissioners were to be concerned with the welfare of the community, and under the terms of the Act their immediate concerns were the provision of water, sanitation, and public street lighting.

In regard to water, one of the first moves the Commissioners made was to stop the practice of ships bringing water casks ashore to be filled at the public wells. These large casks took a very long time to fill, while long queues of women and girls waited with stoups to be filled. Watering of ships was forbidden except before 5 a.m. and after 8 p.m. It was realised, however, that water for ships was a necessity, so a new cistern was constructed at the Ferry-boat Steps at the seaward end of the Shore, specially for the supply of ships, and this cost £850. Ships were charged one shilling per ton for water, but that did not go far towards meeting the cost.

The Commissioners were sore beset trying to make ends meet. The Act made no provision for any regular income for their work, and expenses multiplied. The Big Pipes were by no means big enough. They were led further into the loch to find deeper water, and they were frequently cleared of silt, but in summer the supply simply dried up. In response to repeated urgent appeals Edinburgh granted a two-inch pipe to lead some of the Crawley water for the relief of the port, but in the summer of 1793 there was a drought, and the pipe of Crawley water was cut off: not a drop was allowed to reach Leith until after the emergency. Leith was in a desperate state that summer, for of course the Lochend supply had also failed. Bringing that two-inch

Nicol's Court: Unofficially so-called in honour of Mrs Nicol, an auld wife who lived here and kept a mangle. She took in mangling for which she charged the going rate of 'a farthing a pin'. Nicol's Court and Kirk's barber shop were demolished in 1916 to make way for an extension to Yardheads School.

pipe to Leith cost the Commissioners £1000, and even so, when it was most needed, it was rendered useless.

A Town Tax was introduced to provide an income for the Commissioners, but even with this help their work was always hampered by lack of funds. In 1799 John's Place had just been built — part of the extension of the old town of Leith which matched the contemporary building of the New Town of Edinburgh. Proprietors in John's Place saw no reason why they should not enjoy the luxury of piped water in their houses. They approached the Police Commissioners with a proposal. Briefly, they proposed to pay an annual rent to have water piped into their houses, and in order to get the work done they would lend money to the Commissioners at 5% per annum. The Commissioners jumped at this offer, and eventually every heritor on the line of pipe from Lochend to Leith agreed to pay one guinea a year for piped water, and each agreed to lend the Commissioners £21 to have the work done. The scheme took almost two years to complete. When the great day arrived for opening the stopcocks to the various houses between Lochend and Leith, it was found that no water at all reached the great cistern at the Big Pipes, and the town was soon clamouring for water. The Commissioners then took the difficult decision of forbidding the stopcocks to private houses to be opened until the town's main cistern had been supplied. In the end, however, this was seen to be reasonable, and many other proprietors in Leith got themselves piped water on the same basis of paying a guinea a year in water-tax. Water remained scarce in the port for a long time thereafter. It was only in 1869, when the Leith and Edinburgh water companies amalgamated, that Leith for the first time received an adequate supply and a good pressure of water.

Compared with the difficulty attaching to the water supply, it seemed to the Commissioners that cleaning the streets would be a simple matter. They learned otherwise. There was no difficulty in engaging a local farmer to cart away the heaps of dung and other refuse from the streets; it was quite another thing to persuade the inhabitants to put out their household refuse at a stated time. There were no bins: ashes and household soil had always been thrown out at the householder's convenience. The contractor now arranged for two dung carts to go through the streets at eight o'clock in the morning in winter, and seven o'clock in summer, each provided with a bell which was rung as they went on their way. To start the scheme the town drummer went through the town beating his drum and announcing the new arrangements three times a week for the first three weeks, and once a week thereafter.

This worked well enough for some weeks, but then the dung carts stopped coming, and things were soon as bad as they ever had been. It was then discovered that the farmer, who had paid the Commissioners sixteen guineas for the dung he was collecting, now had enough for his fields, and decided he was better employed getting on with the ploughing than collecting refuse he would then have to sell to some other farmer. The Commissioners cancelled their agreement with him and tried a system of direct labour. They soon found this was too expensive, and eventually got another farmer to take the job. This time the contractor was told that if he failed to keep the streets clear of dung the Commissioners would hire other labour to do so, and charge him with the expense. This seems to have been effective.

Kemp's Close: This ran between Giles Street and Yardheads. Named from Robert Kemp, distiller in Yardheads, and demolished in the Improvement Scheme of the 1880s.

Even with the refuse cleared away, the streets, unmade and unpaved, remained in a near impassable state. Another Act of Parliament, the Second Police Act of 1806, sought to remedy this. It included an order to all proprietors to lay pavement in front of their property — 'flat hewn stones, in such Manner and in such Form as the Commissioners shall from time to time direct and appoint, such Pavement being not less than two or more than six feet in breadth'.

Stretches not built up could be laid with dressed whinstone instead of pavement. The Commissioners then began surfacing the streets with rough rubble, but it was not until 1826 that they agreed to put down square blocks of whinstone — known to later generations as setts. At first these were laid only at the principal crossings, and extended later as money became available.

In the event the townsfolk themselves had to be cajoled, encouraged or bullied into paying for the improvements seen to be necessary, for no public funds were available and the Commissioners were always in deficit. Another serious nuisance in the narrow streets was the many obstructions — outside stairs, projecting shop signs, and buildings not conforming to any reasonable building line. The 1806 act ordered the clearance of all such impediments, but even in the 1860s wheeled traffic was still a great nuisance in Tolbooth Wynd, owing to several projecting stairways still obstructing the passage.

The lack of any street lighting made walking after dark a hazardous exercise. There were no blinds in the eighteenth century. Wooden shutters were used, and these effectively prevented light from houses reaching the street. The Shore was especially dangerous, for there was normally a great agglomeration of rubbish there — ships' gear, offal and the usual potholes — and no protection at the quayside. There were many drowning accidents.

The first move to light the town was an agreement by the Committee of the Police Commissioners in 1771 to put up fifteen lamps, distributed on the Shore and at such other danger spots as might be indicated. Peter Wood was engaged as lamplighter. At twilight he lit the lamps, and at one a.m. he extinguished them. On Sunday 12th March 1772 the lamps were put out and then removed for the summer, as the Commissioners saw no point in wasting oil unnecessarily. The lamplighter also had discretion not to light the lamps on bright moonlit nights. Gradually the rules were relaxed. After a few years the lamps were left burning till daybreak. For many years the Cantore at the entrance to South Leith churchyard was used as a storehouse during the summer months; then, greatly daring, the Commissioners left the lamps in position all one summer, and to their surprise the result was far fewer breakages than had occurred when the lamps were moved in spring and restored to position in autumn.

As with piped water, householders soon began to covet a lamp outside their own front door. It was then arranged that any householder could pay for a lamp with its iron holder, and then the

Williamfield: When the land was enclosed in the 18th century it became common practice to name the fields then formed. When these fields in turn were feued for housing, the field names were often transferred to the houses, as in Springfield, Orchardfield, Seafield. Sometimes the name of the owner of the field or of one of his family was thus perpetuated. Williamfield is in Newhaven Rd.

Commissioners engaged to have it lit every night for a payment of 1s 1d per week. In 1828 the newly formed Leith Gas Company asked permission to lay pipes in the streets in preparation for supplying the town with gas lighting. Gradually gas took the place of oil, first in the main thoroughfares and later in the wynds and closes.

This large and growing community, numbering over 20,000 souls by the end of the Napoleonic War, had no hospital facilities, and public health was an idea still unknown. Before the Reformation the canons of St. Anthony had cared for the sick and aged poor to the best of their ability, and from the early seventeenth century the King James Hospital had provided for about a dozen old women nominated by the incorporations of Maltmen, Traffickers and Trades, while the Mariners made similar provision in Trinity House for their own sick and poor. For a village this was probably sufficient; but in a rapidly growing town, where more and more of the people were engaged in industry with its attendant risks, the old system could no longer cope. Industrial conditions also brought new problems of overcrowding and epidemic disease. Providing adequate care for the sick and aged was a major problem for those governing Leith throughout the nineteenth century.

The first attempt to do anything was made in 1788 when the Humane Society took a room in the Broad Wynd, and installed a bath there with a fire under it and an attendant to keep the fire going. This arrangement was made for the resuscitation of the apparently drowned. As already indicated, drowning accidents were all too frequent. In 1804 a newspaper report stated that in sixty cases dealt with in the sixteen years of its presence in Leith, the Humane Society's bath had enabled forty-eight people to be restored to life. But as the Society depended entirely on public voluntary subscriptions, there was sometimes no money to pay the attendant, the fire went out, the bath was cold, and the next person rescued from the harbour got no help. Nevertheless, despite unreliable support, the bath in the Broad Wynd continued, and the good work went on.

Sickness and poverty and the consequent misery were so common, and the lack of any help so obvious, that in the closing years of the eighteenth century several societies came into existence to alleviate suffering. Among these were the Destitute Sick Society, the Female Society for Indigent and Sick Women, and the Sympathetic Society. These were all wholly dependent on voluntary contributions from the public, and their work was gratefully recognised. Charities like these provided food and clothing, and lodging and fuel, but no kind of nursing or medical regimen. When Dr Andrew Duncan opened a Dispensary in the Broad Wynd in 1816, that was an important advance, for the sick poor were invited to come to the Dispensary for free advice and medicine. This was a service both to the poor and to the medical profession, for students were encouraged to attend at the Broad Wynd and give their services free. In this way they got experience of a great variety of conditions and the spectrum of human need. Situated only a few yards from the Humane Society's bath, the Dispensary consisted of two rooms on the first floor — one a laboratory and consulting room, the other containing a single bed, meant for any patient so far gone that he could not be expected to struggle back home again. Two or more critical cases at the same time could only be accommodated on the floor.

After nine years the Dispensary and the Humane Society

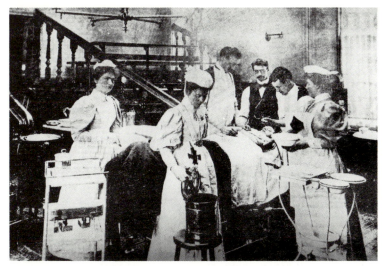

Leith Hospital Operating Theatre c.1910: Specialised facilities hardly existed then. This was simply a room with the blinds drawn to exclude the sun's rays.

amalgamated at 17 Broad Wynd. This was simply an economy measure, for there was no advance in the services offered. The next significant step came in 1837, when a house at 34 Quality Street (now Maritime Street) was opened as a Casualty Hospital. The title is deceptive, as there was no nursing skill available, but at least accident victims could now be given some kind of first-aid in Leith before facing the painful journey to the Edinburgh Infirmary. When the Church of St. Thomas was opened in 1840, a group of almshouses was attached to the church and manse, and here ten aged women suffering from incurable disease were boarded and cared for. The population of the port was now passing the 30,000 mark, and nothing like what the modern world understands by a hospital was available in the town.

When John Stewart of Laverockbank died in 1845 he left £1000 towards the cost of building a hospital for Leith. The gift was conditional on a similar sum being raised by public subscription. This was quickly achieved, and Leith Hospital was opened in January 1851 at a cost of £1878. Again it must be emphasised that this was not what the twentieth century understands by a hospital. Just as the Dispensary and the Humane Society had joined together in 1825, so the Dispensary, Humane Society and the Casualty Hospital were now brought under the same roof to continue their work in more adequate surroundings. Nursing was still rudimentary, the Crimean War and Florence Nightingale being still in the future, but it was soon obvious that the new hospital was quite inadequate to meet the needs of the burgh. The first trained nurse to be employed was Mrs Brown, who came to Leith in 1866 from King's College, London, and was attached to the hospital as District Nurse. The following year an extension to the hospital was opened, and in that same year the Public Health (Scotland) Act was passed, giving Local Authorities power to build their own hospitals. Two years later a Burgh Hospital was opened in King Street, this being simply a conversion of the former Ragged School there. This Burgh Hospital, however, was only opened during epidemics, when Leith Hospital was overflowing, and unable to accept any more patients.

At this period all types of cases were treated together — casualties and infectious disease in the same wards, and attended by the same staff. The hospital doctors were acutely uneasy about this, but a timely legacy of £25,000 from Mr Thomas Williamson Ramsay of Lixmount enabled a further large extension to be added to the hospital in 1873. It was now possible to keep casualties apart from infectious cases, but the same staff did duty in both sections of the building.

It was unfortunate that the hospital established in 1851 was in no sense a public health service. It was a charity, governed by a board of directors, on which the Town Council were represented. As they had no power to direct hospital policy, the Town Council took the view that the funding of the hospital was the responsibility of the directors, and council support remained at a minimum. One consequence was that whereas seven new wards became available with the 1873 extension, only four of these could be used as there was no money to pay the necessary staff. The population then stood at 40,000, and even with all the new wards functioning, the accommodation at the hospital was far short of what was needed to serve the community. And the Town Council still refused to open the Burgh Hospital except in dire emergency.

Miss Sophia Jex-Blake, then in the throes of her struggle to have women accepted as medical students, approached the directors of Leith Hospital in 1886, and they agreed to accept women students into the wards at Leith for clinical instruction; so with all its

Bonnington estate cottages: Newhaven Rd was formerly Bonnington Rd — the road skirting the grounds of Bonnington House. This building, at right angles to the line of Newhaven Rd, is a modernised example of the estate workers' houses.

shortcomings this became a teaching hospital. Two years later a second storey was added to the 1873 extension, but it was now plain to the medical staff that the town required a separate hospital for infectious diseases, and that the Town Council must find the money for it. A long struggle ensued, until the doctors finally announced they would not accept any infectious case into the hospital after 1st October 1891. The Town Council, in a panic, pled for more time, and the ban was not made effective for another two years. Shortly afterwards a smallpox epidemic broke out in the town, and a temporary wooden hospital was erected at the east end of the Links. At long last the Town Council found a site at East Pilton, and a hospital for infectious diseases was opened there on 11th September 1896. (This is now the Northern General Hospital.) It was only then that the general public rallied to the support of Leith Hospital, and from the first years of the twentieth century the strong local interest and support of the hospital never flagged.

In the mid-nineteenth century Leith had a massive housing problem. Old and unhealthy properties abounded. The work of the

Police Commissioners in cleansing and lighting the town a century earlier had not extended beyond the main streets. Wide areas remained entirely without sanitation; lanes and alleys had no causewaying or drainage, and many were so narrow they hardly admitted pedestrians. Provost Watt was taken on a tour of the slums by Dr James Struthers in 1869, and afterwards announced his determination to have all underground dwellings compulsorily closed. He was as good as his word, and immediately set in hand an extensive investigation into the slums of Leith which resulted in the Leith Improvement Scheme of the 1880s. This was a landmark in the development of the town. The area between the Kirkgate and the Coalhill, and between Yardheads and Tolbooth Wynd, was cleared of all the narrow lanes and alleys of labourers' dwellings which had been erected a century earlier in the first years of the Industrial Revolution, to be replaced by wider streets and more substantial tenements in Henderson Street and Henderson Gardens. These streets were named in compliment to Dr Henderson, who was then Provost. It is a pity that Provost Watt, who had set up the whole project several years earlier, has had no street named after him.

The Leith Improvement Scheme was a beginning, but much slum property remained, and continued to deteriorate until the First World War brought all house-building to an end. After the war Leith's housing need was greater than ever before, but by then all the land adjacent to the boundaries of Leith had been acquired by Edinburgh, and it was only through amalgamation with the city that land became available to accommodate Leithers. Thereafter thousands of Leith people in overcrowded conditions were removed to various Corporation housing schemes in Edinburgh.

CHAPTER 6

The Distressed

Poverty, sickness and old age affect every community, and the way in which these troubles are met reveals much about the character of the people. In this respect Leith can be proud of her history. From time to time the port had to cope with exceptionally difficult circumstances, but those who were deprived were neither forgotten nor ignored. Poverty is a relative term, but in many years of scarcity and near famine almost the entire population was well below the poverty line.

In early times the village coped with daily life on a basis of neighbourliness, but the Reformation in 1560 marked a milestone in community care. With no more need to support their own chapels and priests, the incorporations began taking much more thought for the material welfare of their members. Quarterly contributions went into the 'Box' — generally a capacious affair with three locks, so that the Boxmaster with his key required the presence of two Keykeepers before the Box could be opened. This receptacle contained not only cash, but all the documents important to the corporation, including the seal of cause (or charter of foundation), and all correspondence and legal documents affecting the members. The funds were used to pay a small subsistence allowance to any member prevented from doing his work by sickness. Funeral expenses were also paid, if necessary, and the widows of members received a pension. The rules of the various incorporations differed in detail, but these were the benefits to be expected. The 'upset' or entry money varied a great deal between corporations, as did the quarterly contributions; so the amount of the benefits also varied widely.

The presence of the trade incorporations, with their own organised welfare for members, was a very important element in the community life of Leith. As the incorporations had also built the parish church, and took responsibility for its maintenance, and as few families in the port were unconnected with any incorporation, it might be thought that the kirk session were exceptionally fortunate, and would have no worries. The Reformed Kirk in Scotland had a clear view of its responsibility as a national church. The professed objective was to have in each parish a kirk, with a manse for the minister; and a school, with a house for the schoolmaster; and the welfare of the parish poor was the responsibility of the kirk session. In many parts of the country it was found impossible to provide this simple social framework for many years, but in Leith, on the face of things, there should have been no problem.

Nevertheless the organisation of community welfare became both a challenge and a burden to the elders. When the funds of the old preceptory of St. Anthony were finally entrusted to the kirk session towards the close of the sixteenth century, the King James Hospital was built, and between the accommodation there, and at the Mariners' Hospital in Trinity House, the dependents of the incorporations were provided for. Leith's growing importance as a port, however, brought a floating population of seamen about the place, and many of these had no membership in the Mariners' Society. They came from other ports, and other countries. Some of these temporary residents married Leith girls, so there were always families with no claim on any of the benefits provided by the incorporations. Soldiers also were regularly billeted in the town, as Edinburgh was never happy with a permanent military presence, and preferred having the troops quartered at Leith, which was a convenient distance from the city. Another circumstance creating many demands on the kirk session's poor box was the exceptionally large number of beggars in Leith. The law in Scotland confined the kirk session's responsibility to the poor of the parish, and incomers begging in the town were ordered to leave and return to their native parish, where the local kirk session would look after them. It was by no means easy to put this rule into practice. Leith was particularly attractive to beggars, being so near the capital city, and being a seaport with a mixed and constantly shifting population. The variety of activity around the harbour gave abundant opportunity to the begging fraternity. Edinburgh was no more pleased to welcome strange beggars than any other town, and regularly turned them away, so they came down to Leith. The ferry from Fife also brought a constant inflow of undesirables. The law only made provision for the relief of 'the aged poor, impotent and decayed persons', so the able-bodied man without employment had a hard life, and in Leith the 'sturdie beggars' or sorners were a constant nuisance and an occasional menace.

The kirk session issued badges to local beggars which they wore on

Headstone showing Maltmen's crest: Each of the old trade incorporations had its own crest. Examples of these can be seen in the churchyards of South Leith and North Leith.

their left breast, and so they were easily identified. Support given to these unfortunate neighbours was a duty undertaken readily enough, and these licensed beggars were all known in the village, their circumstances familiar to everyone. Any public gathering, however, attracted a horde of supplicants from far beyond Leith. They haunted the kirkyard on Sundays and at funerals and weddings. In 1646, the year following the plague, the kirk session appointed a staffman to take charge of this unwelcome and unruly crowd. Provided with a stout staff, from which his name derived, he had a range of duties which must have been next to impossible to fulfil. He had to oversee the behaviour of the licensed beggars; and he was expected to prevent all strange beggars from entering the churchyard, and to report the presence in town of apparently destitute strangers. It was the staffman's duty to keep the peace at weddings, baptisms, funerals and Sunday services — especially on Sacramental Sundays when the crowds were very large. Householders and others intending to distribute largesse were encouraged and advised to hand what money they meant to bestow to the staffman, who would divide it among the licensed fraternity, and so prevent unseemly scuffles. It really was too much to expect from one man. George Hay, the staffman in 1721, was reprimanded and dismissed by the kirk session for dishonesty. He had been in the habit of keeping to himself most of the money he was given to distribute. By the mid-eighteenth century it became impossible to find anyone to fill the post of staffman, even when the salary was raised from one shilling to eighteen pence weekly. In any case the appointment was only appropriate to a village: it was not feasible for one staffman to officiate effectively in a growing town.

Regular weekly pensions were paid out at the Cantore. This was a small room built over the entrance to the churchyard in the Kirkgate, and was entered by an outside staircase. It was probably built at the same time as the King James Hospital and is first mentioned in the kirk session minutes in 1632. 'Cantore' is an old Scots word for an office or counting-house, but as the payment of pensions occupied only one day in the week, the place came to be used for a variety of other purposes, and in its early days it served as a temporary prison where the kirk session kept petty offenders while waiting for fines to be paid. Here the treasurer attended week by week, paying subsistence money to the poor, the aged and the disabled. There was no standard rate: the contents of the poor box determined the amount to be allowed. If things were going well, widows might be given as much as three shillings a week, which was very good compared with other parishes; but it never lasted long at that level. Each case was considered on its merits. Those aspiring to a place on the poor roll had to petition the kirk session, and their circumstances were closely examined. A widow with several children naturally was given more than a single lady with no children. Also, a young widow was expected to earn at least some money, especially in summer, when there was work available in the fields. Anyone receiving support from one of the incorporations was not normally eligible for a place on the poor roll. The elders had to be hard-faced, as there was never enough money to support all the poor adequately.

At the same time, while the elders had to bear in mind the adage that charity begins at home, there was never any hesitation over responding to a cry for help, even from far beyond the parish, when the need was genuine and urgent. Retiring collections were called for from time to time to help some small village rebuild a bridge carried away in a winter storm. Such a bridge might be that little

Old Restalrig: Until the First World War the village of Restalrig retained its rural atmosphere. The picture dates from the beginning of this century.

community's only link with the outside world. Appeals came from persecuted Protestants in Europe and from congregations in unexpected stress or hardship given permission by the General Assembly to make a general appeal for help. Most frequently it was the hazards of seafaring that brought an immediate and ready response from the congregation. On several occasions the session asked the people for help to ransom a local man held captive by Algerian pirates. The point made was that if the money were not forthcoming, the poor prisoner would either be killed or sold into slavery. On one occasion two Leith merchants informed the elders that they had themselves put up the ransom money for a sailor, and now sought reimbursement. The elders, who could and did spend many hours sifting evidence in some case of petty moral delinquency, made no move to check the genuineness of this appeal. The merchants were at once assured the money would be paid, and a retiring collection was confidently intimated.

In such circumstances the poor box loomed large in the kirk session's thinking. Any possible source of income, however trifling, was carefully investigated. Fines imposed for various misdemeanours went into the poor box; fees for any kind of privilege also went to the poor. In the seventeenth century there were no seats in the church apart from those belonging to the incorporations. Each of these bodies had its own little 'loft' for officials, which in time was extended to accommodate all the members. Anyone else in the congregation feeling the necessity of a seat brought a stool with him. Better-off people, prominent people, those who felt the indignity of acting as their own porters, applied to the kirk session for permission to set up their own seats in the kirk, and the elders, after suitable hesitation and due consideration, granted the privilege, on condition that a suitable sum be donated to the poor box.

Headstones in the kirkyard were also made to serve the cause of the poor. From ancient times local notabilities had been buried under the floor of the kirk, which was then bare earth. The grave was then marked with an inscribed flagstone placed over it. About 1640 the General Assembly ordained that this practice should cease, but that order had to be repeated more than once in later years. It was probably the difficulty of finding any more space under the floor, rather than the General Assembly's injunction, that made it necessary to use the churchyard for all burials. The matter of headstones then became important. The kirk session discouraged the idea. The churchyard was a grazing area, for which the beadle received an annual rent as part of his salary. Headstones would be unsuitable. But families prevented from enjoying the privilege of burial in the church now sought some way of advertising the presence of their dead. Time and again the session refused permission for memorial stones to applicants they did not consider important enough to be granted such distinction. Those who were allowed the privilege had to pay a suitable sum to the poor box. The amount of such a donation was never stipulated: it was left to the generosity of the families concerned. It then dawned on the elders that the new fashion among mourners to have gravestones was something to be encouraged rather than frowned on, for a standard charge for the privilege could represent a steady income for the poor.

For more than half a century a steady stream of fines went to benefit the poor from couples found to be irregularly married. This was a matter affecting Leith probably more than any other place in Scotland, and presented the kirk sessions of both North Leith and South Leith with a particularly frustrating problem. In Scots law it was sufficient for a couple to declare before witnesses that they took each other as husband and wife for the marriage to be legal; but the Church was implacably opposed to such unions, as no record of the transaction was normally made, and the marriage could easily be denied later. Many a girl was left with a baby and no income, when the father denied the union. Again, if the man was in the armed forces he might be killed or drowned, but if the marriage was irregular the wife was not informed of her husband's death: she only heard of it by chance, from others. Unable to prove her marriage, she did not qualify for a widow's pension, and could not even claim a place on the poor roll. With both soldiers and sailors constantly coming and going, irregular or clandestine marriage became common in Leith.

Regular marriage was a ceremony performed by the parish minister, when the details were recorded by the session clerk. Scotland, however, was for so long in a disturbed state, between wars, epidemics and religious differences, that it was not always easy for everyone to have access to a minister to perform a marriage, and various forms of irregular marriage were practised, as well as no ceremony at all. Couples cohabiting, behaving as husband and wife, and accepted as such by the neighbours, would, if it came to a trial, be adjudged as married 'by habit and repute', But this anarchic situation was acceptable neither to Church nor State, and in 1661 the Scots Parliament legislated against clandestine marriage, imposing a range of fines, and three months' imprisonment for offenders. The act was to be operated by kirk sessions and the money from fines applied to 'pious uses within the several parishes'. Those celebrating irregular marriages were also to be banished for life: but in the 'killing times' larger issues were filling men's minds, and the act was ineffective. A second act was passed in 1698 with severer penalties, and the two kirk sessions in Leith began actively pursuing the parties to clandestine unions.

At first about half a dozen cases a year were reported in South Leith, but after the reintroduction of patronage in 1712 this rate more than doubled. Patronage was the system whereby the laird or chief heritor in a parish could nominate a minister to fill the charge without reference to the wishes of the congregation. This was a widely unpopular measure, and a clandestine marriage was a form of defiance of the parish minister. Another steep rise in irregular marriages took place from about 1729, and through the 1730s the average reached twenty-two cases *per annum*, a very worrying development in the life of a village of 5,000 souls. This increase matched the rise of feeling in the Church which led to the Secession from the Establishment in 1733. The first such breakaway in South Leith took place in 1740.

Irregular marriages stood at twenty-five in a year until about 1765, and this took no account of the marriages of Seceders or Episcopalians, all of which were, strictly speaking, irregular, the parish minister having no part in them. This whole tragic business came to quite an abrupt end in 1784, when two acts of Parliament in 1753 and 1781, covering 'England, Wales and Berwick', were extended to Scotland. Briefly, these acts provided that marriages celebrated in churches other than parish churches, and by ministers other than the parish minister, should be deemed valid and legal. By that time the population of Leith was increasing to such a degree that it had become virtually impossible for the elders to be aware of all that was going on in the town in the way their predecessors had known the details of life in the village.

Clandestine marriage was generally discovered when the first child was born and the parents sought the privilege of baptism for their offspring. They came to the session, confessed their fault, and were 'rebuked, exhorted, and ordered to pay the charges'. The fines went to the poor box, the normal fees for a regular marriage were then paid, and the marriage was thus regularised. Then the baby was baptised. When all was said and done, the only ones to benefit from irregular marriage were the poor.

The village of Newhaven was detached from the parish of the West Kirk in Edinburgh (St. Cuthbert's) and joined to that of North Leith in 1631. The Society of Free Fishermen there declared that they would not consent to become part of North Leith unless they were allowed to care for their own poor. The Free Fishermen were not incorporated, but they were organised like an incorporation, and they were of ancient standing, having written records from the sixteenth century. The North Leith elders gladly agreed to the Fishermen's condition, which, of course, removed a burden from their poor roll. The Fishermen then argued that as they were looking after their own poor, they should not be required to contribute to the collection plate in the parish church, and this, more reluctantly, was also agreed. Thereafter, on Sunday mornings, the Free Fishermen set up their own collecting dishes on either side of the road leading from Newhaven to North Leith, and here the Newhaveners deposited their offerings, which were added to the Fishermen's box.

This arrangement appeared to work well enough for a long time, but in 1737, when an infant was found exposed in Newhaven, the Free Fishermen disclaimed responsibility for it. The argument was never settled, but the elders took the child out of compassion. From time to time there were minor differences between the Fishermen and

Inscribed stones in the Martello Tower (1807): After the Irish 'troubles' of 1798 and the Union of Britain and Ireland in 1800, Irish labour appears to have been used in building the Martello Tower. a) The Irish harp. b) 'God Save Ireland'.

the kirk session, but the next serious trouble arose in 1760 when it was discovered that the boxmaster of the Fishermen had made no payments to any of the village poor for two years; and during the same period the members of the Free Fishermen's Society had ceased to make their normal quarterly payments. The Society had received all the Sunday collections week by week, had paid nothing out, and had apparently abrogated its responsibility for its own poor. The kirk session sent a committee of investigation to Newhaven, and as a result of its findings the collection of monies and the distribution of pensions to the poor in Newhaven was taken over by the elders. The session soon found this a cumbersome and time-wasting procedure, so in 1768 the Fishermen again took over the handling of their funds, but under the supervision of the kirk session, who received reports on the operation of the fund from time to time.

Once more there was peace and quiet, but fresh trouble erupted in September 1814 when Elizabeth Grant was added to the North Leith poor roll, and granted a pension. When this was reported to the kirk session, one elder said Elizabeth Grant was a Newhaven woman, who ought to be sustained by the Free Fishermen. On enquiry this was proved, but the Fishermen refused to take her on to their roll, as she was not a member of the Society and was not related to any member. It then emerged that the Free Fishermen had never accepted responsibility for anyone not connected with their Society. The difficulties with the elders over the years had arisen from a misunderstanding. Like any incorporation, the Free Fishermen had always considered their responsibility as limited to the families of their members. The kirk session had from the beginning assumed that the Fishermen were taking care of all the poor in Newhaven. In the seventeenth century it probably made little difference which view was adopted, as there were then very few in Newhaven not connected in some way with the Free Fishermen. By the end of that century, however, the pattern was beginning to change, as labourers in the ropeworks and glassworks, and farm workers in the vicinity were added to the fisherfolk. Through the eighteenth century the population continued to diversify. There now ensued a long period of argument while the elders tried to persuade the Fishermen to extend their responsibility; but the Newhaveners held out, and the matter was only resolved in 1828, when an assessment for behoof of the poor was introduced, and all responsibility in the matter was removed from the kirk session.

By this time, oddly enough, North Leith had long possessed its own

Grill to foil grave-robbers: This example from South Leith churchyard indicates the trouble and expense families were at to prevent the unwelcome attentions of the 'resurrectionists'.

poorhouse, while South Leith, much more populous, had none. The opening of the Edinburgh Charity Workhouse at Bristo in 1753 was almost immediately followed by a flood of beggars descending on Leith, and the Leith bailies issued warnings to the people not to give to any but the local licensed beggars wearing their badges. The Leith incorporations, led by the Traffickers, met with the ministers to investigate the possibility of having a poorhouse built in South Leith. Lack of money defeated this project; but in North Leith matters went better. A session minute of 29th April 1760 is interesting:

> The Moderator represented that as the Neighbouring Parishes were all getting Poors houses, it would be convenient for this Parish to think of getting one, that they might be free of the great number of begging Poor that are every day strolling about.

The idea was to put all the begging poor under one roof, provide for their maintenance, and so stop the nuisance of street begging. By August 1763 the kirk session were able to take possession of a house built for this purpose in the Citadel area. Newhaveners were excluded as a rule, although an exception was made in the case of one woman, the kirk session reserving their right 'to dismiss her at pleasure'.

Contrary to the reputation later acquired by poorhouses or workhouses, when even the destitute resisted efforts to take them there, the eighteenth-century poor eagerly sought admission to the Poorhouse. Discipline in the house was strict, and anyone guilty of a misdemeanour was liable to immediate ejection, to make way for the first in the queue awaiting admission. In 1815:

> Widow Meldrum in the poor-house acted in a very imprudent manner, getting drunk, and striking the other lodgers there. The session ordered their officer to turn her out of the house.

Yet the hard face of official charity was a mask that had to be worn because of the shortage of funds and the continual rise in the number of the poor. Privately, a good deal was attempted through philanthropy. One procedure repeated from time to time after a poor harvest and the certain expectation of a hard winter was for a group of Leith merchants to club together and buy a cargo of oatmeal which they stored until scarcity and high prices cut off the poor from that staple of Scottish diet. Then the meal was sold cheaply to the needy. On at least one occasion the elders in North Leith issued a peck of meal free, in addition to the normal dole, to everyone on the poor roll. While Christmas was not formally recognised by the Church, and Christmas Day was an ordinary working day for most people, the season was privately observed, and in both South and North Leith a free issue of coal was usually made to the poor at Christmas-time.

Leith for long counted within its vicinity a group of villages or hamlets, each with its own community sense. Newhaven may have been the most fiercely exclusive of these small enclaves, but Hillhousefield, on the site of Pitt Street and Trafalgar Lane, Bonnington with its mills, Calton at the southern end of South Leith parish, and Restalrig, the ancient hub of the parish, all cherished their own identity and their own view of life. Restalrig in particular never forgot its ancient status as the centre of the parish, and for ever hankered after doing things in its own way, regardless of South Leith. Shortly after Leith was legally confirmed as the administrative centre of the parish by an Act of 1609, the heritors and local farmers in Restalrig formed their own independent charity under the odd title of 'the Restalrig Society of Friendly Contributors'. The idea was for the contributors to purchase a set of mortcloths which could be hired for funerals, the proceeds being used for relief of the local poor. It was not a success, apparently because the contributors expected the hiring fees to repay the outlay on mortcloths before the poor could begin to receive any benefit. Having become moribund for a period, the Society was reconstructed in 1726 and did rather better. The only benefit the Restalrig poor got from it, however, was cheap burial, but the Society moved on to other activities for the benefit of the community. A similar society in Calton also organised cheap burials, but it petered out before the end of the eighteenth century.

The urgent drive for Navy recruits during the Seven Years' War (1756-63) brought the Marine Society to birth, and after that war this organisation remained, to continue its good work among poor boys in Leith. The work of the Marine Society is best summed up in this extract of a minute of their meeting on 12th July 1764:

> *Resolved*: That we will, as usual, select those objects who are the most pitiable, and in the lowest stages of human misery, preferring the orphans of sailors and soldiers, if such should appear, and particularly such boys in general, whose parishes are not ascertained, and who are in most danger of being bred up as vagabonds to beggary or robbery; and that we will place them out as young; and as speedily, after they apply to us, or we discover them, as possible, to all businesses relating to the sea; as mariners, fishermen, and particularly fishermen in new fisheries, boatmen of all kinds, shipwrights, shipjoiners, anchor smiths, ropemakers, sailmakers, blockmakers, riggers, caulkers, boatbuilders and oarmakers, in the merchants service.

Selected boys were given clothes and settled as apprentices, their fees being paid. Others were medically examined, issued with clothes and bedding and given free passage to London, where they were sent on board ships of war, serving as officers' servants while they learned to be seamen.

The ending of war with France in 1815 was followed by a long industrial depression. Unemployment figures rose alarmingly, for a horde of ex-servicemen, many of them disabled, swelled the ranks of beggars on the streets of Leith. Writing of this period, Robert Chambers commented:

> The number of poor in Leith appears to be very great. They are crowded into all the various mean alleys, and loiter on the streets in all directions beseeching alms from the passengers, or melting them into compassion by more indirect appeals from fiddles and other instruments of music. The favourite station of these musical mendicants has been from time immemorial the thorofare of Leith Walk, where at one time every loathsome object was daily exhibited to the passengers.

Like other places, Leith always had its 'daftie' — generally more than one. The daft laddie or lassie was always kindly treated and evoked more compassion than the 'sturdie beggar', who could be an unmitigated nuisance. When the simpleton grew up, however, he sometimes became a public menace, and the kirk session had still another problem on their hands. When Edinburgh acquired its Bedlam or Asylum adjoining the Workhouse at Bristo, this was the nearest place to Leith for the reception of lunatics. Once the patient was admitted to the asylum, it was then a problem finding maintenance for him from the parish poor box. A minute from North Leith session in 1788 makes this very clear:

> The Moderator produced to the Session a letter directed to them from Mr Richard Richardson... setting forth that unless the Session would give their obligation for the maintenance of Alexander Philp's son, carpenter, now in Bedlam, that he would immediately be turned out.

Two or three parish lunatics confined over a long period imposed a heavy burden on parish resources.

In early times there was little ceremony attaching to burials in the Presbyterian Church, but by the beginning of the nineteenth century this was changing, and there were three recognised classes of burial — hearse, shoulder-high and spoke funerals. Class distinction here was obvious. Hearses had to be paid for, and it was cheaper to hire four or six bearers to carry the coffin shoulder-high. When the corpse was borne to the grave on a couple of spokes the family poverty was proclaimed, but that was all the expense the kirk could afford for the burial of the poor.

South Leith finally acquired a poorhouse in 1850 — just a few months before Leith Hospital was built on the adjoining site. It remained for over half a century, until in 1907 a new house was opened at Seafield, and the inmates were transferred there. The hospital then acquired the site of the old house, cleared it, and formed Taylor Gardens, the purpose being to admit more light and air to the hospital. The Seafield Poorhouse in course of time has been upgraded and transformed to become the modern Eastern General Hospital.

The business prosperity of late Victorian Leith was accompanied by widespread poverty. The community divided into three sections. At the top were the business and professional people, whose income was more than adequate, and whose work was assured, although often enough hard and demanding. Then came the new and growing class of white-collar workers, whose earnings were modest, but sufficient to maintain a reasonable standard of living all the year round. Thirdly, and most numerous, were the general labourers, dockers and tradesmen who had just enough, when working, to provide for their wives and families with no margin. Bad weather in winter meant unemployment for these men, for longer or shorter periods during which there was no income at all and starvation was a dire possibility.

This massive poverty was seen with sympathetic eyes, but it was widely accepted as inevitable — especially as Jesus had said, 'The poor ye have always with you'. With many people this counted as the last word on the subject. At the same time there was plenty of philanthropic feeling in the town and in the churches. Dorcas societies and clothing clubs flourished for the benefit of the poor, and in 1872 a soup kitchen was opened at the Coalhill, where, during the worst of the winter, free meals were dispensed by a committee of ladies from South Leith Parish Church. This began in a very small, tentative way, but was maintained through the years until in 1892 the *Leith Burghs Pilot* reported that 160 to 170 meals were being served daily, and that almost 22,000 meals had been served in the previous winter. The report goes on:

> The children are the very poorest, and are sent for the most part by the town missionaries... There are also a few very poor old people... But for the kitchen many a child would have fared very badly indeed in the cold winter when the parents had no work, or had wasted the means which should have provided comfort in the home...

One most effective development in providing assistance for the poor in Leith in Victorian times was the institution of the House of Call in 1872. This model lodging house was a great boon to single working men. The building in Parliament Street was extended over the years until by 1909 it had 150 beds. Men were accommodated here for $3\frac{1}{2}$d, $4\frac{1}{2}$d or 6d per night, and some confirmed bachelors made the House of Call their permanent home.

The introduction of health insurance and old age pensions just before the First World War, and of unemployment benefit after 1918, transformed the social scene, and while unemployment remained high in Leith between the wars, the threat of starvation each winter receded. Since then the Welfare State has created such a social matrix that today we no longer have any knowledge of poverty in the port such as former generations took for granted.

CHAPTER 7

The Young Mind

Education for some Leith boys was almost certainly carried on in the Preceptory of St. Anthony; but this was not done with any literary or scholastic goal in mind. The boys were taught singing in a sang schule, that they might assist at the services in the chapel of the preceptory. It would be enough to be able to read music and the accompanying words. This training was considered important, however, and after the Reformation the kirk session of the parish church continued the sang schule, appreciating the value of a trained choir to lead congregational singing. When a vacancy occurred in 1610, the elders urged the minister to find a new master for the school 'with all possible diligence', and recommended writing to Aberdeen 'for ane man may both reid and teache musick'.

Education for all was an ideal pursued by the Reformed Kirk, so after 1560 the sang schule was expanded to become the vulgar school — the school where the vulgar or common tongue was taught, along with music. The kirk session encouraged parents to send their boys to school, and by the later seventeenth century girls also were being schooled. It is interesting to note that at the Vulgar School it was the Scots tongue that was taught, the change to English apparently being made only in the eighteenth century after the Act of Union in 1707. It then became known as the English School, and here all children whose parents were prepared to pay were given an elementary education — reading, writing and arithmetic.

In addition to this coaching in the essentials, there was also available from the time of the Reformation a grammar school education. The 'grammar' was Latin grammar, and indeed Latin was the only subject taught. The course at the Grammar School was intended as a preparation for entrance to the University, where all the teaching was in Latin. Latin was the universal language of scholarship, so familiarity with that language was essential for an academic education. It must none the less have been a dreich regimen for young boys. Pupils entered the Grammar School at the age of nine, by which time they were expected to be able to read and write. Five or six years at the Grammar School were sufficient preparation

Leith High School, 1806-96: The Grammar School of Leith spent the 17th century in the vaults of Trinity House, the 18th century in the King James Hospital, and the 19th century in the High School.

for the University, which most boys entered about the age of fourteen.

The Grammar School met in the vault of Trinity House (the predecessor of the present building) which the kirk session, as governors of the school, rented from the Mariners. The roll normally stood at around thirty, so the whole school could meet in one room. The arrangement with Trinity House lasted throughout the seventeenth century, but in the early eighteenth century the Mariners intimated that they intended raising the rent, and the elders refused to pay. The Grammar School was removed from Trinity House and accommodated in the hall or common room of the King James Hospital, where the incorporations of Maltmen, Traffickers and Trades met to do their business. Here the Grammar School remained until 1806, when Leith High School was built on the Links.

Whether any boy ever enjoyed his Grammar School education must be open to doubt. In summer classes began at 6 a.m. and continued all day till 6 p.m. with two breaks of one hour for breakfast and dinner. Winter compelled a shortening of the school day — not to benefit the pupils, but to save coal and candle. It was the mid-eighteenth century before this timetable was curtailed, and classes then ran from 7 to 9 a.m., 10 a.m. to 1 p.m., and 3 till 5 p.m. The School was under the direction of a Master, who was paid 200 merks a year, which he supplemented from the fees. When the school roll increased beyond thirty, the Master was allowed to employ an assistant, known as the Doctor. In that situation the Master was paid 300 merks, and was expected to pay the Doctor 100 merks; but that seems to have been at the Master's discretion, depending on how much he valued the Doctor's services.

In 1729 the Master of the Grammar School was Thomas Kirkwood, who proved a failure. Under him the roll dwindled, and he was summoned before the kirk session to answer charges of gross negligence and unseemly behaviour. Kirkwood's defence included a description of his teaching methods:

> I've no fixed time for prescribing the lessons and examining them. I humbly beg leave to lay before my reverend patrons my method of teaching, viz — Every Monday morning I take an account of the sacred lessons which were presented the Saturday before, together with the repetition of the Catechism and the notes of sermon. And, in the afternoon I prescribe a lesson in their rudiments, grammar and authors, and appoint the boys to give an account of them the next day. And likewise I prescribe Mondays night a general pense [exercise] which I take an account of next morning immediately after prayers are said; the superior classes having with the same pense either a theme or a version [translation] to write, and so on from day to day. This method was for most part observed excepting when some things fell in my way to divert it... It has always been my practice to punish the boys that were absent at the hours of convening unless they brought from their parents a written excuse mentioning that they were necessarily detained.

The Grammar School continued throughout the eighteenth century in the King James Hospital, but that building became damp, the accomodation had always been limited, and with the increased population a number of private schools were scattered about the town. At an earlier period no one could open a school in Leith except under licence from the kirk session, but this strict supervision had had to be relaxed in the changed conditions of the Industrial Revolution. Only a small number of boys were ever intended for the University, but a liberal education was sought by many families for their

Leith Nautical College: This building in Commercial Street was the first purpose-built nautical college in Scotland. The College moved to Milton Road East in 1972.

children, and this could be had in private schools. Usually the teacher professed only one or two subjects, which he taught in his own house. If he was reckoned to be good, he attracted sufficient pupils to give him a living off the fees. When the new school building was erected on the Links, it was not intended for the Grammar School only. Here was accommodation for several teachers to operate independently, offering a variety of subjects all taught under one roof. The teachers rented their own rooms in which to teach their own subjects. The public saw the new building as a group of schools, and for many years the building on the Links was known as the Leith High Schools.

The old Grammar School had been governed by the kirk session, but the new building was under the management of an extraordinary body of trustees, consisting of the two ministers of the parish church, the two resident magistrates, with three nominees each from the Police Commissioners, the Maltmen, the Trades, the Traffickers and the Mariners. None of these trustees knew anything about education, and the resultant chaos almost put Leith High School out of existence midway through the nineteenth century.

There was no curriculum in the modern sense. Parents decided which subjects their children should study, and sent them to the appropriate classes, paying the required fees. The parents also decided when to finish their children's schooling. Most of the pupils, however, went through all the courses the school had to offer. There were four main classrooms. Mr Bayne taught Classics and Mr Foggo took the English class. These two were for long regarded as being still the Master and Doctor of the Grammar School. Mr Rankine instructed a class in Writing and Arithmetic, and Mathematics was taken by Mr Ingram, who had come over from Trinity House to the new school.

The teaching of Mathematics in Scottish schools was pioneered by the Mariners at Trinity House, who in 1680 appointed a 'professor' to teach mathematics to the sons and apprentices of shipmasters. The subject taught was the mathematics of navigation, and the first to hold this post was George Drennan, who was followed by some remarkable men. In 1699 John Man took over, and he soon began the annual publication of 'Prognostications' for Edinburgh. These were weather forecasts based on astronomical observations and calculations. In 1704 he issued separate forecasts for Leith. By agreement with his employers Man also ran a private school in Leith, and in 1719 his successor Robert Lauchlan also applied to the Mariners for their permission to take private pupils for mathematics at his own home. The Mariners thought so highly of Mr Lauchlan that they made him an honorary member of Trinity House — a rare distinction and compliment. Later in the eighteenth century Alexander Wood, successor to Lauchlan, produced the first map of Leith to be based on a proper survey which he had himself carried out. That was in 1777: six years later Wood was succeeded by Alexander Ingram. This appointment, however, was not confined to teaching navigation, for he also had to add writing and arithmetic to mathematics. It was Ingram who made the transition to the new High School, where Mr Rankine relieved the maths teacher of the extra burden of writing and arithmetic.

On the ground floor of the High School a spacious hall was flanked on the right by Mr Bayne's classroom, and by Foggo's English classroom to the left. An iron staircase circled the wall of the hall, leading to a similar classroom arrangement upstairs, where Messrs Rankine and Ingram taught their respective classes. At the rear, downstairs, was a small room which eventually became the rector's

Balmerino House, Kirkgate: An early 19th century view, showing the dress of the Grammar School boys.

sanctum; while upstairs the room at the rear was used as a music room. There was also a basement which for many years was rented out as a bonded store. No doubt the income from rent was welcome, but it was an unfortunate arrangement for a school. Many years later one former pupil recalled that when the bungs were removed from casks for the convenience of the Customs Officer inspecting them, some of the schoolboys managed to insert straws through the bung-holes, sucked the whisky, and made themselves tipsy.

Mismanagement by the trustees was the main reason for the reputation of the school being steadily eroded in the first half-century of its existence. As already explained, it was really a group of small schools under one roof, and no effort was made to co-ordinate the activities of the independent classes. There was no headmaster and no overall direction of the school. At first there was neither janitor nor cleaners. Each teacher was responsible for cleaning his own room and the section of corridor outside it, and this led to continual bickering. Fees in the Grammar School had been paid quarterly, with a special gift to the Master at Candlemas. There was also a separate charge for coal money. After some years on the Links these payments were all commuted into four quarterly fees. When a janitor was appointed,

Dr Andrew Bell: Founder of the Madras system of education. His provision for a school in Leith was a major benefaction to the town.

instead of his receiving a proper salary, each pupil had to pay him sixpence a quarter. This was to be collected from the children by the teachers, but as some teachers were forgetful, it soon became the janitor's duty to collect his pay from each child attending school. To eke out his earnings, the janitor was allowed to sell biscuits to the children, but he was reprimanded for extending his stock to include gingerbread and sweets.

Another consequence of there being no headmaster was that the methods of teaching and the school books used continued unchanged from the days before the school on the Links was built. This was a serious drawback, for new books and new ideas of class discipline were rapidly coming into use in other schools. Parents becoming aware of this began sending their children elsewhere. In the 1820s and '30s the roll varied between 150 and 250, although the building was intended to accommodate 585. In 1848, under the Leith Municipal and Police Act, the High School Trust became vested in the Magistrates and Town Council, with the two ministers of South Leith Church. This ought to have been an improvement on the former inchoate governing body, but in fact there was no effective change. The Town

Council even refused to subscribe towards much needed repairs at the school. Elsewhere town councils had always maintained their own grammar schools, of which they were very proud, but the history of the Grammar School in Leith had been different, and all that the local council contributed was £10 *per annum* for school prizes.

The standing of Leith High School was now quite peculiar. It was known to be old-fashioned, and was avoided by better-off people who had bright children. The roll continued to dwindle, and in 1855 the Town Council, much against their will, had to advance £20 to make up the salary of Mr Oswald the Classics master. At the same time the school enjoyed a high social reputation in Leith. The old Grammar School had always stood high in local esteem, and many remarkable men had been counted among the pupils and teachers. By the mid-nineteenth century, however, the High School, unlike the old Grammar School, was co-educational; and the pupils belonged to families whose ambitions leaned rather in the direction of social prestige than of academic achievement. Here is one man's recollection of that period from forty years on:

> Oddly enough, we of the other schools laid aside every vestige of jealousy of the High School when its annual examination came round. We stood in groups around the gate as the cabs came up with daintily dressed young ladies, and we admired the trim, gentlemanly lads who had been taught to walk erect and comport themselves with dignity... And then how we cheered them when they came out, some of them laden with gloriously gilded books and bedecked with flowers in their short, tight-fitting jackets that you see in old pictures of the period... Then the young ladies — how daintily they stepped out of the carriages, displaying 'clocked' stockings and buckled shoes, with black elastics, describing a St. Andrew's cross over the most elegant of insteps! It was a royal day, in which the old jealousies were as completely forgotten as if they had never existed.

The tide began to turn in 1863, when the trustees at last decided to appoint a rector to take charge of the whole school. Had this decision been made in 1806 when the building on the Links was first opened, there would have been a very different story to tell, but at least in Peter Macfarlane the school was under a very able man. It was the more to be regretted, then, that the rector was never given a real chance. The reactionary spirit still prevailed. Neither the rector nor any of his staff were paid any salary, their income depending entirely on fees; and the roll of the school was far too low to produce a living wage from fees alone. After six years Mr Macfarlane resigned, and there followed a vacancy which lasted for a year. During that interval George Watson's Boys' College opened in Edinburgh, and Leith High School pupils drifted away so fast that when William Macdonald was appointed as the second rector, there were only twelve pupils left. Macdonald soon pulled the school together, and it was not long before 150 were in attendance again. But this was a very small number to be coming from a town of some 60,000 inhabitants. The school had no endowments, and no income apart from fees. It was impossible to contemplate the kind of changes and developments necessary to bring the school into line with the well-endowed Edinburgh schools, and it was fortunate that the Education (Scotland) Act of 1872 brought Leith School Board into being. With considerable relief the Town Council in the following year agreed to transfer the High School to the care of the School Board. The council's record in regard to the school was a miserable tale of tight-fistedness and myopia, but there was a swift improvement once the School Board had taken over.

The number attending the High School now rose so quickly that by the 1890s the place was overcrowded. In 1888 Leith High School became Leith Academy, and the change was welcomed in the town as evidence of a new democratic feeling. The name of the Leith High School had carried overtones of snobbery and exclusiveness. The change in name marked not only the dawn of democratic feeling in the school, but also the beginning of academic ambition. The High School was demolished in 1896 and replaced by the building that is now Leith Primary School. Ten years later numbers had so continued to swell that the upper storey of John Watt's Hospital was taken over by the school, and soon the whole of Watt's Hospital became part of the Academy. When Leith amalgamated with Edinburgh in 1920, there were also classes in a large army hut erected in the playground. Watt's Hospital was replaced in 1931 by Leith Academy Secondary School, and the 1896 building then became the Junior School.

This succession of Grammar School, High School and Academy affected only a minority of the children of Leith. Long before the High School became co-educational there had been schools available for teaching girls. In the late seventeenth century there was a 'woman's school' in Leith — that is, a school taught by a woman, who trained girls to read, write and 'work stockings'. Stocking-making was a home industry widely engaged in by women at that time, and teaching a school provided a widow with a livelihood. These private schools were conducted under licence from the kirk session. When Anne Inglis in 1727 sought permission to open a school to teach girls to read and sew, she had to satisfy the session 'that she was well satisfied with the Governments of Church and State, that she had and owned [i.e. accepted] the Confession of Faith, and the Assembly's Catechism, that she attended the ordinances in the Church, and would enjoin her scholars so to do'. Mrs Oliphant on the Shore set up a boarding school for girls in 1754, and advertised her venture in the *Edinburgh Evening Courant:*

> Mrs Oliphant designs to set up a SEWING SCHOOL for White & Coloured Seam, also Washing & Dressing. And Ladies who will be so good as to entrust her with their Children, may depend upon having them carefully waited on; And those who incline to send in their Children from the Country, may have them accommodate with Lodging & Boarding; together with the best Advice Mrs Oliphant is capable of against the Extravagancies of Youth. She likeways proposes, That those Scholars that are Boarders with her shall be taught Writing & Arithmetic, within the House at her Charge — Likeways Ladies or others, who will be so good as give her in Seams, shall have them carefully done. Those who incline to favour her in this, may call at Wm. Oliphant's Bulking Master on the Shore of Leith, near Barnie's Nook.

In 1806, the year the new High School opened on the Links, Mrs Wilson, at her house in Charlotte Street, was instructing girls in 'Plain and Fancy Work, English and French, Writing, Arithmetic and Drawing, Music and Geography', as well as 'paying scrupulous attention to the morals of those entrusted to her charge'.

All this was education acquired for the payment of fees. Most children in Leith then received no education, or very little, partly because their parents could not afford fees, and partly because facilities were quite inadequate. When the Grammar School vacated the King James Hospital, no more old women were admitted, but the premises, damp and verminous as they were, at once filled another role. The rising concern for the sick poor at this period also extended to the multitude of poor children around the streets and waterfront, and the idea of free education began to take shape as a form of charity. The King James Hospital was taken over as a testing ground for a Charity School. The enterprise had to be launched and maintained entirely on voluntary subscriptions, and it was a remarkable success. Thus encouraged, the Committee of the Charity Schools began to look for better accommodation, and in 1813 the Leith Boys' and Girls' Charity Schools moved into their own premises in King Street.

About a hundred boys moved with the Charity School from the Kirkgate to King Street, but they were not just riff-raff. About half of them had fathers in the armed forces, or in domestic service, and most of the others were the sons of widows. They were poor, but not neglected. On an even lower level of the social scale were the youngsters nobody wanted, who slept rough, who relied for food on begging or stealing, who dressed in rags and especially infested the docks and waterside. The Seamen's Friend Society, formed in 1820, concerned itself with the needs of seamen and their families. The Seamen's Academy offered instruction to masters, mates and men, that they might be in some degree equipped for life at sea. No other formal course was available, and this experiment was enormously successful, attracting hundreds of men. And for the poor children of the waterfront three separate day schools were organised, and accommodated on board a hulk moored in the Queen's Dock (later known as the West Old Dock). By 1828 these schools had rolls of 210, 120 and 185, and the hulk on which they were taught was known as the Floating Chapel, as it was used for seamen's worship on Sundays.

The next development in local education came with the setting up of Dr Bell's Trust. Andrew Bell, while a missionary in India, devised a system for teaching large numbers of children with a very small qualified staff, by using monitors as pupil teachers. On his return to Scotland he set about applying his 'Madras' system of education in this country. Dr Bell was a wealthy man, and by his will he directed substantial sums of money to various towns in Scotland to establish schools devoted to the Madras system. In this way Leith received about £10,000. A trust was formed in 1831, the Magistrates and Masters of Incorporations being the trustees. Various disputes prevented anything being done for some years, but there was no lack of enthusiasm for the new school, and before any site for a building was found, the school was started in the Masonic lodge in Constitution Street. Eventually a site was obtained adjacent to the Relief Church in Great Junction Street (now St. Thomas-Junction Road Church) and a building was erected.

Education at Dr Bell's School was not free, but the fees amounted only to a few pence per week, and the roll increased steadily. Music and sewing classes were introduced in the 1850s, and in 1861 children attending the Charity School in King Street were also drafted into Dr. Bell's. This came after long and painful discussion among the trustees of both schools. It was felt that the Charity School was an anachronism, and that the Madras system could be applied to a wider range of Leith children. Fees at Dr. Bell's were very modest, but even so they were adjusted to the parents' ability to pay, and were sometimes waived altogether. There were no fees at the Charity School, but the standing principle would apply to children transferring to Dr. Bell's. Fees would not be compulsory. Clothes presented another problem. Pupils at Dr. Bell's were adequately, if poorly, clad: at the Charity School some had fairly presentable clothes while others were in rags. The trustees finally agreed to admit to Dr. Bell's 'such of the Charity School children as are fit objects to receive gratuitous education and are at the same time properly clothed'. They saw a clear distinction between the 'respectable poor' and the others, who were not just poor, but destitute. They said they bore in mind the fact that there was in the Charity School 'a class of children who are apparently better fitted for a ragged school'. So only the children from King Street who were properly clothed were transferred to Dr. Bell's School. Eighty-two children were added to the roll of Dr. Bell's in this way in 1861, and as more and more pupils appeared at the beginning of each term, a second Madras School was opened in South Fort Street in 1870. This school lasted only fourteen years, for the Education (Scotland) Act of 1872 made it necessary for several new schools to be provided, and the school in South Fort Street was found too small to be serviceable, so it was closed.

The old King Street premises now became the Leith Ragged Industrial School. An Industrial School had been opened in Edinburgh in the 1840s in an attempt to find a solution to the problem caused by children being arrested and charged with street begging, stealing and other offences. The law directed young offenders over the age of seven to be committed to prison. Industrial Schools were intended to reform such youngsters by giving them some kind of industrial training, instead of a term in prison. In this way it was hoped to be able to find them some kind of useful employment. These schools were soon known as 'Reformatories', and the school in King Street quickly flourished, to the extent that in 1869 it moved to purpose-built accommodation in Lochend Road.

Watt's Hospital: Erected in 1860 as a home for old men, on the site of the former Golf-house, it became an annexe of Leith Academy from the early years of this century. Demolished in 1928, it was succeeded by the Leith Academy Secondary School.

This school for juvenile delinquents eventually became a source of pride and joy in Leith. The Industrial School had a brass band which, after the conversion of the Links to a public park in the 1880s, played regularly at the bandstand on summer evenings, taking its turn with other local bands. Old Leithers still remember the procession from the school on Sunday afternoons to the service in South Leith Church; and year by year, in Edwardian times, the Industrial School band headed the long crocodile of children with tickets for 'Hislop's Trip' wending its way up the Kirkgate to Leith Central Station yelling 'Hurrah for Mr Hislop and his happy, happy band' to the tune of 'John Brown's body'. The Industrial School was followed in the Lochend Road premises by St. Anthony's Roman Catholic School.

   With the passing of the Education Act, Leith School Board took over the management of eighteen schools in the port, and there were also twenty-three private schools. Most of these latter were small concerns, but a few were well known and well attended, such as Walker's, Laing's, Foreman's and the Kay-Gardner Schools. These establishments succeeded or failed in direct response to the personality and ability of the teacher in charge, and men like 'Daddy'

Laing and John Kay were widely respected and long remembered.

John Kay started teaching in a room in Charlotte Lane in the 1820s. Later he removed to 107 Constitution Street, where his school was considered the best in Leith:

> Did a boy fall behind in his lessons at another school, he was sent to Kay's. Did he get out of hand and beyond the discipline of another school, he was sent to Kay's. It was not the master only who 'licked' him into shape, it was the other boys as well.

Mr Gardner started as Kay's assistant. He went on to become head English master at Bathgate Academy, but on Kay's retiral he was persuaded to return to Leith, and the school became the Kay-Gardner School. In the 1850s and '60s it was without question the best school in the town, and when it moved to 2 Links Place it became known as Leith Academy. Mr Gardner retired when the Education Act was passed, the school closed, and the premises were taken over as the School Board Offices. Some years later the name 'Leith Academy' was assumed by the High School.

Another significant development was the opening of Holy Cross Academy in 1907. This began as a training college for Roman Catholic teachers, and it was housed in Afton Lodge, 208 Ferry Road, which had been the residence of the Rev. Dr Hutchison, minister of Bonnington United Presbyterian Church. The house stood in almost four acres of ground, which ensured room for future expansion. For almost seventy years Holy Cross Academy provided secondary education for Roman Catholic children from an area far beyond the bounds of Leith.

The first Merchant Shipping Act came into operation on 1st May 1855, and one consequence of this measure was the establishment of navigation schools in various ports. Until then there had been no formal training for ship's officers. Boys went to sea as apprentices, and learned their trade while serving on board. Under an able and interested master the youngsters could be well trained, but this did not always happen, and there were no recognised tests of skill and knowledge. The Merchant Shipping Act sought to remedy this, but it was difficult to find capable and efficient instructors.

Leith Navigation School was opened on 20th September 1855 in a room belonging to the Mariners' Church in Commercial Street. In attendance were four shipmasters, two mates, twenty-six seamen, eight ship apprentices, twenty trade apprentices and eleven day scholars. Under John Newton as Master the school made a good start, but after two years Newton left to take charge of the Glasgow Navigation School. Mr Burchill was then conditionally appointed as Newton's successor, as he had not yet qualified; and in the autumn of 1858 he failed to pass the examination for the Navigation Certificate. In the meantime the school had dwindled from 103 pupils in attendance when Newton left, to only thirty. The Government Department of the Board of Trade then proposed closing the school, but the local committee would not hear of it. Burchill remained for another year and then found himself another job — by which time all the adult students had left and only three small boys were in attendance. The school then closed, but the committee were grimly determined to have a navigation school and continued the search for a suitable Master. Eventually, after many disappointments, the secretary in Leith received a letter from the Government Department recommending a young man for the job, whom the Government would be prepared to pay. It was like an answer to prayer.

When James Bolam came to Leith in January 1861 he was twenty-one years old, and had been Assistant Master at Trinity House Navigation School, Newcastle. He had already qualified by passing the Navigation School Teachers' Certificate on the highest grade in every subject, and he was to spend over sixty years in the post he was now taking up. He was allowed to accept boys from the age of ten who were intended for a seafaring life. He had to pay attention to their religious knowledge, and was obliged to pay the managers of the Navigation School £30 *per annum* to cover rent and overheads. Whatever then remained from fees he could keep as salary.

After a year the Navigation School removed to the top flat of No. 60 Tolbooth Wynd, which was a building on the site of the old Tolbooth which had been pulled down in 1820. A few years later another move was made to 2 Commercial Street, and again in 1882 the school was transferred to 14 Dock Place. This was a warehouse block redesigned to Mr Bolam's specifications — a fact indicating the growing success of the school. After March 1865 examinations for engineers in British steamers became compulsory, and this was a strong encouragement to young seamen to attend the Navigation School.

Apart from his main occupation James Bolam had other interests. He became actively involved with the Leith Science School, instituted in 1875 — forerunner of Leith Technical College. As the managers of

Newhaven Parish School: Long abandoned as a school, this building still stands behind Newhaven Parish Church.

the Science School had no funds, the enterprise was wholly financed from fees. By 1885 pupils at the Science School were being offered Machine Construction and Drawing, Steam Engine, Applied Mechanics, Architectural Drawing and Building Construction. The school met in the evening in the High School. Mr Bolam also organised an Art School, housed in a building which was later cleared away to accommodate Junction Bridge railway station. The art classes were then continued at Leith Technical College.

James Bolam's main ambition, however, was to have a purpose-built Navigation School. He nursed it for years without much hope; but when one of the managers, Mr John K. Wishart, died, and left £200 to the school, Bolam used the money to start a building fund. The value of the work undertaken by the Navigation School was increasingly recognised by shipping interests in the port, and two influential men joined the board. James Currie, head of the Currie Line, became a strong supporter of Bolam, and the Board met regularly in the office of the Currie Line. A second powerful addition to the management of the school came with Christian Salvesen, who was added to the Board in October 1881. But the very success of the school was involving the managers in ever-increasing running costs, so that the dream of a new building was becoming fainter, when an unexpected piece of good fortune altered prospects. After the 1872 Education Act the School Board had taken over both of the Madras schools in Leith; fees were abolished, and the staff were paid by the Government. The income from Dr Bell's Trust now had no object. In 1885 the Royal Endowed Schools Commission considered what was to be done, and after receiving a memorial from James Currie, W.D. Thorburn and the Rev. Dr. Mitchell, representing the Navigation School, Leith Science School, and Leith School Board, a large share of the income from Bell's Trust was directed to the Navigation School.

Another new source of income now appeared — known to Leithers as the 'Whisky Money'. When the Local Taxation (Customs and Excise) Act of 1890 was passed, a certain amount of Customs and Excise duties raised locally was allowed to be spent locally, in Scotland. £40,000 was set aside from this for police superannuation; £40,000 for relief from payment of fees in state-aided schools; and £15,000 to pay for medical officers and sanitary inspectors. The residue could be used by town councils for technical education locally. The Navigation School applied to Leith Town Council for a contribution from the 'Residue Grant' as it was called, and received £100 for the ensuing year. A small contribution also came from Edinburgh Town Council, and this 'Residue Grant' continued until 1909, when, following the Education (Scotland) Act 1908, the grant was standardised on the basis of what had been paid in the preceding year. During that year someone must have been working on behalf of the Navigation School behind the scenes, for the grant was then suddenly increased; Leith Town Council contributed £250 and Edinburgh £50, so from then on the Navigation School was assured of an annual income of £300 from these sources.

In the meantime the Dock Commission had given the school a site in Commercial Street for the new building, and the work was put in hand, with Mr William C. Laidlaw as architect. The managers agreed to change the name of the school when the move was made to the new building, so on 4th February 1903 Leith Nautical College was opened by Lord Balfour of Burleigh, the Scottish Secretary, who then promised increased Government help for the College, stressing that 'We consider this institution one not merely of local, but of national importance'.

The 'sphere of influence' — i.e. the catchment area of the new

Leith Academy Secondary School: Opened 1931 on the site of John Watt's Hospital — originally the site of the Golf-house. An etching of *c.*1935.

College — was agreed with the Government to be the coast ports between Fife Ness and Berwick-upon-Tweed, including the whole of south-east Scotland south of the Firth of Forth. Leith Nautical College was the first building in Scotland provided solely for the purpose of nautical education, and James Bolam remained at the helm. After years of pressing for it, he had the satisfaction of seeing a Marconi wireless installation set up in the College in 1913 — providentially just in time to fit in one year's instruction in its use before the outbreak of the First World War in 1914. Mr Bolam retired in 1923 at the age of eighty-four, but lived to see an extension for Marine Engineering opened by the Rt. Hon. Viscount Novar in 1927. A second storey was added, and opened in 1931 by Rear-Admiral the Hon. W.S. Leveson-Gower, but the old Master had died two months earlier at the age of ninety-one.

An incomer to Leith at the age of twenty-one, James Bolam became one of the port of Leith's greatest townsmen, and the Nautical College, even on its new site on Milton Road, remains his lasting memorial.

CHAPTER 8

The Environs

The port of Leith that amalgamated with the city of Edinburgh in 1920 was clearly marked on the map, but this boundary was of fairly recent origin. The history of Leith is concerned with the land enclosed by the parishes of South and North Leith, extending along the coast from Fishwives Causeway to Wardie Burn. Southward, the area included part of the modern city of Edinburgh, as the parish boundary of South Leith marched with the parishes of Duddingston and Canongate, to include Restalrig, Jock's Lodge and Calton; and North Leith, from 1631, included Newhaven. It was not until 1826, with the passing of the third Police Act, that a boundary for the port was defined. This extended from the Citadel, along Great Junction Street and round the Links to Seafield, but seven years later, with the establishment of the independent Burgh of Leith, the boundary was moved southward to Pilrig Street, took in the old North Leith Parish as far as Craighall Road, and went by Lochend to Seafield. This restrictive definition of the area of Leith has therefore existed for not much more than a century and a half. For the centuries before that, the wide area of countryside encompassed by the two parishes was closely involved with the life of the port.

Even in the 1770s the area of Yardheads and St. Anthony's was still considered to be outside the port proper. The Shore was then the centre of Leith, and when Alex. Wood's map was published in 1777, the population stood at around 10,000, and much of what the twentieth century considers to be Old Leith was still open fields, nurseries or gardens. The onset of the Industrial Revolution in the mid-eighteenth century not only changed the appearance of Leith, covering open ground with rows of workers' dwellings; it also changed the lifestyle of most Leithers. The generation who were active in 1750 were villagers, closely engaged with work on the land, or involved in earning their living from the sea. By contrast, their grandchildren were town-dwellers, many of them still with rural and maritime connections, but engaged in sedentary occupations to a degree their grandparents had never known.

The Links afforded only the roughest grazing, but further inland, where the ground sloped gently upward, the land around Leith was fertile and productive. Early farming methods were inefficient and wasteful, and only improved when the land was enclosed. Throughout Scotland enclosure proceeded gradually in the course of the eighteenth century, but in the vicinity of Leith the ancient infield and outfield system ended exceptionally early, for by the start of the century farms were being worked by individual tenants, although there were few dykes or hedges as yet. When the decision to enclose was taken, it needed several years for fences, dykes or hedges to be created. This transitional period brought special problems, and for almost forty years the Burlaw Court of Leith existed to deal with these difficulties.

On 20th July 1715 a petition was presented to Edinburgh Town Council from occupiers of land 'lying near to the citie of Edinburgh and toun of Leith and upon the highwayes and roads thereto', complaining that they had 'suffered considerable damnadges by stealing and carying of great quantities of corns from the feilds in tyme of harvest', and that their crops had also been trodden down 'by men, horses and other beasts' and that their grass had been 'eaten up and Distroyed by straingers cattell'. They therefore craved a remedy. Action following on this petition saw the setting up of a Burlaw Court from Lammas 1716. Burlaw (or Byrlaw) was the local custom or law of a township or rural district whereby disputes could be settled without going to the law courts. The authority of the Burlaw Court was established by common consent of those holding land within the district, and it had binding force within that area.

The Burlaw Court of Leith had authority over an indefinite area. Eastward its jurisdiction ended at Restalrig, for that village had its own Burlaw Court, but in other directions the bounds were vague. From time to time farmers applied to have their lands entered with the Burlaw Court, which gave them membership of the court, and the benefit of its statutes. The original petition to the Town Council had been given in by 'the inhabitants of Leith, possessors of the lands belonging to Herriot's and Trinity Hospitals, lying on the east side of the Walk leading from Edinburgh to Leith'. 'The Walk', be it noted, was not at that time a thoroughfare from the city to the port, as the North Bridge did not exist then, but the farms of Upper and Nether Quarryholes were entered on the books of the Burlaw Court, so at the start the court served the area between Leith Walk and Restalrig Road, but before long a much wider district was included. The farm of Windlestrawlee at Goldenacre, for example, was later entered on the books.

Meetings were held between March and October, and for at least the first nine years of its operation the court met in the open air at the Duckat Yeard. This name, like so many other local names of the period, has disappeared from Leith, but it may have been in the vicinity of Hawkhill. At an earlier period the Beir Hill seems to have been in this same area. From at least the sixteenth century the Beir (or Barley) Hill was where petty customs on goods travelling to Leith were collected, as well as the mettage rates for weighing grain and flour. By the eighteenth century the Beir Hill was but a dim memory and the very name was probably forgotten. Another farm mentioned in the records of the Burlaw Court was Newmains, situated near the foot of Lochend Road. This was probably the same as Coatfield Mains, which later in the century was farmed by John Pew; and a nearby cottage was long known for some obscure reason as Laugh-at-Leith.

After the early years in the open the members of the Burlaw Court began to look more to their comfort, and, except in warm weather, met in John Clephane's tavern, situated about the east end of the present-day Duke Street. Clephane himself was a keen golfer, and the Honourable Company of Edinburgh Golfers on Leith Links met in this same howff for their Saturday night dinner. The court met under the authority of the two Bailies of Leith, and the clerk to the court was Alex. Home, the town clerk. The Burlaw Court was not a charge on public funds, but had to be self-supporting. Income was derived from fines and fees. Each member paid an admission fee of 3s (15p) per acre of all the land he entered with the court, as well as an annual levy of 1s 3d (6p) for each ploughgate, which was probably 104 Scotch acres. This complicated system appears to have been altered in 1730 to a quarterly payment of 1s (5p) by each member.

From the subscriptions paid it is possible to gain some idea of the size of farms around Leith in the first half of the eighteenth century. Several members paid for half a ploughgate, representing around fifty-two acres; one ploughgate was common; two ploughgates less common; and there were only two cases paying for three ploughgates. By the end of the century farms were larger — from 100 to 300 acres. Special rates were provided for gardeners (presumably market gardeners) who entered smaller plots of land.

In the early years bounds were marked by march stones, and

Hermitage House (formerly Lady Fyfe's House): Demolished in the 1880s to make way for East Hermitage Place.

complaints were made about these stones being moved by night; cattle allowed to stray over a neighbour's land also brought many protests. Cows and sheep were then herded through spring and summer, to prevent damage to growing crops; but once the harvest had been gathered in, the animals were allowed to range freely over the stubble. Gradually, however, dykes were built — dykes rather than hedges, for a young hedge was no barrier to wandering kye. It is noticeable that the earliest dykes appear to have been built around grass parks, and the practice of allowing free range to animals over the stubble was gradually phased out. This began with the introduction of a fee for the grazing — so much per animal grazed. As harvest proceeded neighbours would book grazing for so many beasts. Stubble grazing kept the animals going until the onset of winter, when they were taken in and had to get by on next to nothing until the spring, if they were not slaughtered when they came off the stubble.

Farming was largely arable. Two or three horses and the same number of cows, with a few ducks and hens, made up the livestock on the average farm around Leith. This was enough for the family's needs and for the work of the farm. Milk did not travel well, and there was very little winter feed for cattle. Dairy farming and beef breeding were practices still far in the future. True, the records of the Burlaw Court mentioned large flocks of geese from time to time, but these belonged not to farmers, but to brewers and fleshers who could fatten the birds from waste products to which they had access.

The usual crops were oats, barley, wheat, peas and beans. Wheat was not widely grown, although it was commoner in the Lothians than elsewhere in Scotland. Wheaten flour was a luxury comestible, and by the mid-century the art of winter-sown wheat was well understood. There is mention of wheat sown in December, and of wheat growing in November. This became possible with the extension of dykes and the enclosure of cattle on permanent lea. Arable land could then be safely ploughed and sown in autumn.

The number of gardeners increased steadily, and there were notable experimenters among them. In April 1741 a case was brought to the Burlaw Court by William White, a gardener at Ironside, Abbeyhill, against a Canongate brewer, for allowing three hens 'to pick up the complainer's sown peas, turnips, carrots and other small seeds'. This is the first mention of turnips in the Leith area, and they were obviously much prized seeds in White's garden. It was to be many years before turnips were accepted as an addition to the housewife's resources, but it was not so long before their value as winter feed for cattle was recognised, and this was a major step forward in animal husbandry.

With the extension of enclosures fewer cases were brought to the Burlaw Court. Meetings in the early days were weekly or fortnightly, but gradually the attendance of members fell away. More than one meeting was adjourned for lack of a quorum, and the last entry in the books is dated 8th June 1752.

Field work was something most working folk in Leith were involved in until after the Napoleonic Wars. As already indicated, the kirk session took account of this when paying pensions from the poor fund. A widow comparatively young and able-bodied, with a young family, would be supported through the winter, but in summer she was expected to be able to earn a living from casual work in the fields. Everyone could find work at the harvest. Apart from that there was weeding, which was women's work, and many Leith girls and women spent weeks in early summer hoeing in the fields and market gardens. The country was frequently at war, the press gang was active, and male labourers were in short supply. Normally the harvest was worked in teams of five — two girls and three men. Two men went ahead with scythes, and the first girl gathered armfuls of the cut stalks. The second girl made straw bands for binding the sheaves, while the third man bound the sheaves and stooked them. This team could harvest two Scotch acres in a day's work — which was equivalent to $2\frac{1}{2}$ English acres. Barley had to be cut with the sickle, as it tended to lie badly, making it difficult to cut with the scythe. When the sickle was used, a team of nine workers was needed, but eight of them could be women or boys. In the latter years of the French wars men were hard to come by, and all crops were then cut with the sickle, as women could not easily handle the scythe.

The working day began at six in the morning and continued till six in the evening with a half-hour break for breakfast and a two-hour interval at midday. The harvest worker had a Scotch pint — almost an English half gallon — of porridge, with a mutchkin ($\frac{3}{4}$ pint English) of buttermilk. For dinner he had a fourteen-ounce loaf of bread and half a Scotch pint ($1\frac{1}{2}$ pints English) of beer. Supper was the same as breakfast — porridge and buttermilk.

It was an era of agricultural improvement. Not only was the land gradually enclosed with dykes and hedges, but the farm buildings and the cottages of the hinds or workers were also greatly improved in the course of the eighteenth century. When the mediaeval arrangement of farm buildings disposed around the laird's house for protection was abandoned, together with the joint cultivation of arable infield, the first farm steadings — the farmer's mains — were erected in a square. The farmer himself occupied one side — a single storey with two or three apartments under a low ceiling, an earthen floor and very small windows. All the buildings were low, for they were built of turf and stone alternately, or else stone with clay for mortar. Roofing was either of thatch, or thatch mixed with divot. A second side of the steading consisted of the barn, in which the roof timbers were built into the wall at the foundation to give more stability, but the barn was no more than five feet high. On the opposite side were the byre and stables. There were no stalls for the horses, and they fed together. Cattle, not being so placid, were tethered to posts. The fourth side of the square was taken up by the farm cottages, and in the middle of this quadrangle was the dunghill.

Agricultural development was more advanced in Lothian than almost anywhere else in Scotland, and the second half of the eighteenth century saw a remarkable transformation in farm

St. Triduana's Well: A famous centre of pilgrimage in the Middle Ages, this well is now preserved under a stone canopy at Restalrig Church.

buildings. The primitive steading was replaced by a stone-built farmhouse, generally with two stories and five or six apartments in addition to kitchen, dairy, larder etc. The improved barn was eight to ten feet high and twenty feet wide, often divided into two sections for threshing different kinds of grain; and over the threshing-floor there was commonly a loft for storing grain. The byres and stables were divided into stalls, and the fourth side of the square was either open, affording a view from the farmhouse, or else a low wall provided some privacy. The centre of the square — the close — formerly a dunghill, was now generally taken up with a straw-yard where cattle overwintered, and this was walled in to ensure free access to the house. The entire steading was stone-built and the farmhouse roofed with slate while the rest of the buildings were tiled. Some farmers still favoured thatch, but this was rapidly going out of favour, as it was dearer than tiles, it harboured vermin, and it was too liable to fire.

Instead of forming one side of the steading, the farm cottages in the late eighteenth century were generally built about a hundred yards away, in a row. These also showed much improvement on the accommodation of a generation earlier. The old-style cottages of mud and stone were very low, as such walls could not easily support the weighty roof of thatch and divot. Buttresses of unhewn stone helped to prop up the walls. The floor was earth, and one end of the cottage was occupied by a huge chimney, projecting over the floor-space. This generous proportion of lum was intended to ensure that all the smoke escaped through the chimney, but in fact it rather ensured that a good deal of rain came in. The only other light in this clay biggin came from a tiny window. The new type of cottage was stone-built, seven or eight feet high, with straw thatch, and some had a timber floor and a ceiling. Floor space in one of these improved dwellings was sixteen or eighteen feet square. In the 1790s this type of cottage could be erected for £15.

While this kind of straightforward farming was to be found around Leith, as at Restalrig, Lochend, Coatfield Mains, and the home farms or mains of Pilrig, Hillhousefield and Bonnington, there were other townsfolk who, because of their business as bakers, brewers, fleshers or innkeepers, regularly fed flocks of geese or poultry or fattened pigs. They could use or sell the produce, and marketed their stock even as far away as the north of England. Also, in the later eighteenth century a growing number of market gardeners cultivated ground between Leith and Edinburgh.

Marketing vegetables was a trade that developed slowly. Potatoes were grown in the garden of Pilrig House in 1741 as a novelty. Three years later they were tried out as a field crop, and by the end of the century they were to be found on every farm. This crop, however, was exclusively grown within six miles of the city, as transport costs from further away cancelled out the profit. Other garden vegetables did not make the same progress, although gardening enthusiasts were setting up commercially in nursery grounds of from two to six acres. As already mentioned, turnips were tried out at about the same time as potatoes, but only found favour as cattle feed. About 1780 swedes were introduced, and were considered to be better, as cattle ate them more readily. Cabbages were grown in small quantities, as few people would eat them, but kale was widely grown, even in cottage gardens, as it was a universal favourite for the soup-pot and required little manure and less attention. Carrots, parsnips, root crops generally, met with stiff resistance from the public. The most profitable garden crop was rhubarb, which was grown, not for the stems, but for the root. One stool of rhubarb, grown on for five years, was reckoned to yield 24 lbs of root which, when dried, yielded 3 to $3\frac{1}{2}$ lbs. This was sold to apothecaries for a good price, as it was a valuable medicine.

Stewed rhubarb was unknown, but one observer wrote: 'As an ornamental plant, it is hardly equalled; and in rapidity of growth when in the flower, is unrivalled by any known in this country'.

The great development in farming practice and the improvement in farm buildings was matched by changes in outlook, in lifestyle, in dress and manners. Even farm labourers sought at least some education for their children. Reading, writing and arithmetic were taught for a total of 3s 10d (19p) per quarter, and the ploughman's bairns might get one or two quarters' schooling in the year, when field work was slack. The ploughman was paid partly in money, partly in kind. On a typical farm he received £6 per annum and sixpence ($2\frac{1}{2}$p) a week. He had two pecks ($17\frac{1}{2}$ lbs) of oatmeal every week, and during harvest, breakfast and dinner were supplied in the field. Also he was given two pairs of shoes in the year, and all his coal was delivered free.

In the late eighteenth century older men still wore the blue bonnet, but young ploughmen, like their sisters, were disdainful of their parents' style of dress. On Sundays the young man would be seen in a blue coat, velveteen vest, corduroy breeches, white cotton stockings and calfskin shoes, with a white muslin fringed cravat and a hat. The style is well known through pictures of Robert Burns. Girls were no longer content with the homespun and homemade clothes their mothers wore. Harn (a coarse linen) in summer and plaiding (flannel) in winter might serve for rough work and household duties, but even the tradesman's daughter now cast longing eyes on the dress materials offered for sale in the Edinburgh shops. This tendency to break with tradition in matters of dress was matched by new attitudes. While Edinburgh society was enjoying its Golden Age in philosophy, letters and science, the working class was shrugging off ancient superstitions. Witches and fairies were no longer taken seriously; instead there was a naive persuasion that anything appearing in print must be true. On the other hand old customs and ceremonies retained their popularity. These, too, might in time pass away and be forgotten, but Leithers, both in the port and in the landward parts, still maintained many ancient forms of etiquette and followed time-hallowed customs at christenings, marriages and funerals.

The marriage celebration required the presence not only of the bride and groom, best man and best maid, but also the appointment of Master Household. This functionary was chosen from among

Bonnington Mill and Lade: In the last stage of dereliction before being cleared away. Like so much of Old Leith, it has succumbed to the developer.

friends or relatives for his jocular manner, his tact, his ability to make a party go. Master Household organised the seating at table, organised the succession of toasts and speeches, and generally managed the whole proceedings. That, of course, was the grander kind of wedding. When the ploughman married his lass there were no lavish wedding presents in the modern manner, but all the guests contributed in money or kind for the young couple's welfare, and in this way from £10 to £20 might be gathered. This went a long way towards furnishing a cottage, since all that was needed was a bed, two chairs, a table, a chest of drawers and a clothes press. The height of ambition for such newly-weds was to possess a clock, and all this furnishing could be achieved for an outlay of £10 to £12.

The land around Leith had long been popular with Edinburgh citizens looking for pleasant country or seaside quarters either instead of or in addition to the cramped conditions of tenement dwelling. The coast from Leith to Granton was dotted with large villas in ample gardens. The Citadel area was a fashionable district, and the slopes behind the Links were progressively feued as Leith merchants and shipowners sought the amenities of the country within short distance of their places of business. In the half-century from 1770 to 1820 the acreage of land around Leith given over to market gardening almost quadrupled, and the crops taken from these areas of intensive cultivation confirmed the fact that while vegetables found slow acceptance, fruit abounded — apples, pears, gooseberries and currants. One section of Giles Street was long known as the Green Tree — the tree in question being an ancient, massive pear tree. The *Edinburgh Evening Courant* on 8th June 1815 reported ripe cherries being sold from a shop at the Green Tree, and this was offered as evidence of the exceptionally mild weather, as the cherries had been grown in the open garden, without glass, at Hermitage House. But as far back as 1754 one gardener had recommended Leith as a suitable place for propagating bulbs — a trade which, even then, was largely monopolised by Holland. Leith, he claimed, had an excellent climate, and also 'plenty of Cow dung, sand, and Tanner's Bark, and a dark, grey, sandy, Virgin Soil'.

Sir James Elphinstone became the first Lord Balmerino in 1603, and in the following year he purchased the lands of Restalrig from the Logan family. In 1746 the sixth Lord Balmerino was beheaded on Tower Hill for his part in the '45 Rebellion, and the forfeited estates were then purchased by an agent of the Earl of Moray, who was a nephew of the late Lord Balmerino. By the end of the eighteenth century the Logan lands were either being farmed, cultivated as market gardens, or had been feued for housebuilding. The principal landowner in South Leith was then the laird of Pilrig. The name Pilrig, it is conjectured, originated in mediaeval times, and indicated a peel tower built on the low ridge overlooking the gentle slope

Entrance to the Citadel: The pend is original: the house above is early 19th century. This is the view from inside the Citadel looking towards Johnston Street.

towards the sea. Oral tradition has it that Mary of Gueldres, Queen of James III, had a country house at Pilrig in the fifteenth century. Certainly the Monypenny family were living there in 1506, and remained for three or four generations. The house was bought in

1623 by Gilbert Kirkwood, an Edinburgh jeweller and goldsmith, who appears to have taken the old building down, replacing it with an L-shaped house in 1638. Gilbert did not enjoy his new place for long, as he seems to have been a victim of the plague in 1645, and was succeeded by his son, who did not remain there long either before selling the house. It then had a succession of owners until it was bought in 1718 by James Balfour. Balfour was a merchant in Leith with varied financial interests who invested heavily in the Darien Scheme, and lost everything. Eventually he received compensation from the Government, and so bought Pilrig House. The family continued to be involved in the business life of the port, and in 1828 another James Balfour added to Gilbert Kirkwood's mansion, filling in the angle of the L with two large rooms, which became the dining and drawing-rooms, and a hall. He also added a laundry and wash-house, a wine-cellar, dairy, and extra servants' bedroom.

The Restoration of the Monarchy in 1660 was greeted with great relief and joy in Leith, since the years of the Commonwealth had been a miserable time of armed occupation and many restrictions. No one then foresaw the thirty years of religious controversy that were to follow: instead, both royal and municipal approval was given to the Leith Races, and several new industries were begun in a small way, with limited success. It may have been in a spirit of celebration, during the brief euphoria of those days, that the great avenue of trees was planted at Pilrig House. A triple row of beeches on either side of a wide grassy ride led from Leith Walk to the house. At the time of this planting Leith Walk had barely come into existence, and the rampart and ditch constructed by General Leslie's army in 1650 was still in its original state. No doubt the intention of the Pilrig proprietor then was to have had a proper entrance made. Two small cottages, one on either side, at the Leith Walk end of the avenue, were probably intended as quarters for lodge-keeper and gardener. Double entrance gates and a drive would have made an imposing approach to the house, but the scheme was never completed. The times were difficult after the initial rejoicing at the Restoration of King Charles II, and the house changed hands several times. Leith Walk itself remained in a very rough state for more than a century after its construction. When James Balfour took over in 1718, he had other priorities, so the great entrance gates in Leith Walk were never built. When the house was enlarged in 1828, the James Balfour who was then laird had the entrance moved to Pilrig Street, and the entrance on Leith Walk was

Lochside Cottage: This is now Lochend Road South. The house with the projecting porch was the last thatched cottage in Leith, according to John Russell.

closed with a railing. At that time a wide herbaceous border was made on both sides of the drive leading from the house to the Pilrig Street gate. This was known as the Flower Avenue, and it became a well-known 'sight'. The only unfortunate feature in the landscape then was the Broughton Burn, which flowed along the other side of Pilrig Street before turning and meandering through the grounds of Pilrig House on its way to the Water of Leith. It had become so heavily polluted that there was a public outcry about it in the 1840s, and when Rosebank cemetery was being laid out the Broughton Burn was led into a culvert.

In the course of the nineteenth century the Pilrig lands shrank progressively as more and more lots were feued. The Stanwell nursery and orchard occupied space next to Junction Road Church and Dr Bell's School in the first half of the century, but in the 1860s a large area was occupied by the tenements in Bonnington Road, Burlington Street, Tennant Street and adjacent streets. About the same period the ancient beech avenue was showing signs of disease. Most of the trees were felled and eighteen tenements erected — called

Balfour Street as a compliment to the family in Pilrig House. Then in 1894 an agreement was reached with Leith Town Council to convert another portion of the estate into a much-needed public park. At the other end of the Pilrig lands 6½ acres were acquired in the eighteenth century and the house known as Stewartfield was built, on the site now covered by the Comet warehouse. Here, in the first years of last century, lived Hugh Veitch, the town clerk of Leith.

On the north side of the Water of Leith stood Bonnington House, with lands stretching to Newhaven. What is now Newhaven Road was called Bonnington Road until well past the middle of last century, for this followed the boundary of the Bonnington estate. East of this area was the land attaching to Hillhousefield House. Until well into the nineteenth century Hillhousefield was also the name of a village or hamlet on the Hillhousefield lands. It was only in Victorian times that North Leith lost its rural aspect. The old parish church of St. Ninian was closely surrounded by the cottages of local tradesmen. The original churchyard of North Leith occupied the site selected by General Monk, head of the occupying Commonwealth troops in the 1650s, on which to build a citadel. With a promise to provide another burial ground, Monk went ahead with the building, and for some years North Leithers had to share the churchyard in the Kirkgate with South Leithers, until a new churchyard was laid out on the river bank just a few yards upstream from the church. And after all the time and labour spent on it the Citadel was only completed in 1657 and occupied for a few months before being abandoned after the death of Oliver Cromwell and the collapse of the Commonwealth.

The area of the Citadel became the fashionable quarter of Leith in the late seventeenth century, when the Duke of Gordon set up house there — the only openly acknowledged Roman Catholic household in Leith at that period. North Leith's importance in the years that followed stemmed from the fact that all local shipbuilding was established on that side of the river. After the appearance of John Paul Jones with a threatening fleet in Leith Roads had alerted Edinburgh to the relatively defenceless state of her seaport, Leith Fort was built in 1780, and sheltering under the Fort wall on the east side a curving line of brick-built houses provided quarters for the officers of the Fort and their families. These were most elegant, well-proportioned little two-storied houses in the English style, and brick-built housing was then a novelty in Scotland. This was London Row, and it was a great pity that the redevelopment of the Fort site after the

Second World War led to the demolition of this unique feature of Old Leith.

Apart from the industrial area around the shipyards, North Leith remained open country until the burgeoning commerce and trade of South Leith created a need for new housing — housing especially for the new class of white-collar workers. This kind of building began to appear soon after the end of the French war. Ferry Road, Trafalgar Street, Pitt Street, North and South Fort Street and Albany Street (now Portland Street) were occupied by shipmasters, schoolteachers, and various professional men. North and South Fort Street were so named as being north and south of the toll on Ferry Road. As the century advanced, North Leith was built up, not so much with tenements, of which relatively few appeared, but with small terraced villas. The horrendous slums of South Leith were never matched in North Leith.

Despite its 80,000 population at the beginning of the twentieth century, Leith had only a small number of better-class houses. Apart from Trinity, which was within North Leith, the only other salubrious area was the land around the Links, where a number of large villas appeared — Pirniefield House, Seacot, Prospect Bank House, Hawkhill House, Hawkfield, and Claremont House. The best-known of these in the eighteenth century was probably Lady Fyfe's House. Yet this mansion did not survive for much more than a century. First erected in 1754 on ground now covered by East Hermitage Place, Hermitage House was advertised as having a 'Kitchen, 12 Fire Rooms, Garrets, Closets, and other Conveniencies, all neatly and substantially finished, with a Stable, Hay loft and Brewhouse, and other Offices. The Possessor may also have three Pavilions presently used for Summer Lodgings, with the Kitchen Garden and Wall-fruit Trees, and from 8 to 20 acres of fine Grass Ground, well watered and fenced...' Ten years later the Countess of Fife bought the house, set in Hermitage Park. Perhaps she was attracted by one special amenity mentioned in the advertisement of 1764, namely 'a pipe of fine water brought into the kitchen and stables'. As there was no public service of piped water in Leith at that time, this was a special feature of Hermitage House. The advertisement continued: 'The place has short and easy access with Edinburgh, and is known, upon the whole, to be one of the most pleasant and most commodious for accommodating a large family of any in the neighbourhood'.

The grounds of Hermitage Park occupied the area between Lochend Road and Restalrig Road, stretching south towards Hawkhill. The park was known and admired for the fine hardwood trees growing there. Lady Fyfe did not remain at Hermitage for long; the house had various owners until its final demolition in the 1870s. William Cochrane, of Cochrane, Paterson & Co., corn merchants in Constitution Street, was the last owner-occupier. In the 1850s he changed the name from Hermitage House to The Hermitage. In 1868 the Edinburgh Co-operative Building Company purchased five acres of Hermitage Park and built rows of small terraced flats there — a design the same company repeated in various districts throughout the city. These were named Oakville, Ashville, Thornville, Woodville, Woodbine, Elmwood and Beechwood Terraces, in reference to the fine trees that had formerly graced the site. A few years later the eastern half of Hermitage Park was also built over and the streets there were named Cornhill and Ryehill, in memory of the corn merchant who was the last to live in The Hermitage. The rest of the land of Hermitage Park was built over in the 1880s after the removal of the big house, although before that happened the strip along Restalrig Road was built up and named Lindsay Place, after the Provost of that name, and Hermitage Hill — names which have disappeared under the modern inclusive name of Restalrig Road.

CHAPTER 9

By Land and Sea to Leith

Leith's ancient standing as the principal port in Scotland lends special interest to the routes and lines of communication giving access to the place. For hundreds of years the village was a trading centre. Ships were loaded there with goods from many parts of Scotland, and set sail both coastwise and overseas to a great variety of destinations. In particular the city of Edinburgh, for so long the feudal superior of the port, lay a mile and a half away, and the traffic route between the two places was of great importance from early times.

Early in the twelfth century, so far as is known, Berwick, Roxburgh, Stirling and Edinburgh were established as the original four royal burghs, and by royal charter Edinburgh acquired possession of the harbour and mills of Leith. This was an asset of great value, which, if the trade of Leith prospered, could provide lucrative income for the city in time to come. Moreover the royal burgh had the freedom of foreign trade, whereas the port itself was deprived of that privilege. Access to Leith and its harbour was obviously of immense importance, and from those early days Easter Road was a main thoroughfare. This was the direct route from the city to the sea. Leaving the burgh of Canongate by the Watergate, the traveller had only a few yards to go to cross into South Leith, as the boundary ran along the north back of Canongate (the modern Calton Road). Thence by Abbeymount the road led north to the Links and so to Leith. The cluster of cottages which then comprised the port had no thoroughfare, and no need of one; but Edinburgh seems to have been determined to emphasise her right of access to the harbour by making a clearance through the jumble of houses. This became the Burgess Close, where the city merchants built their stores and counting-houses.

Easter Road bore its name from an equally early, equally indeterminate time, for there was always a Wester Road between Edinburgh and Leith, although it never seems to have been so called. It led from the city, by the villages of Broughton and Bonnington — a pleasant, but markedly longer, route. This was known as the Langgate. After the Reformation the Bonnytoun Port gave access through the town wall for those approaching by the Lang-gate. This roundabout way never carried anything like the traffic to be found on the Easter road, or on the later Leith Walk, but there were mills at Bonnington, and a bridge over the Water of Leith which carried the road from Edinburgh to Newhaven.

It is not easy to realise the lack of overland transport facilities in Scotland long ago. Until the second half of the seventeenth century wheeled traffic was rare, as the state of the roads, even in the lowlands, made it impracticable. The bulk of long-distance transport was by sea; otherwise, across country, the packhorse was used, and heavy loads were moved short distances by carts with runners. The incorporation of Porters of Leith specialised in 'tursing' — carrying heavy bundles on their backs. Two hundredweights was nothing out of the way for such a load. A section within the Porters' society were known as 'Rollers', whose business was to roll casks. Before the advent of the wheeled cart, it is said that casks of wine were moved from the port of Leith to Holyroodhouse by a gang of Rollers standing ten yards apart. The first man rolled a cask ten yards, where the next Roller took over and rolled it to the third man, while the first man walked ahead to a new position ten yeards ahead of the last man in the gang. If this tradition is true — and certainly the existence and work of the Rollers is beyond doubt — it describes a most laborious method of transport.

The road itself was not a made road, but simply a beaten-out track with neither bottoming nor road metal. Deeply rutted, the large potholes were often full of rainwater and dangerous, especially after dark. Deep mud abounded in winter, while in summer dust blew everywhere. It was hard going for the elderly or disabled. Early in the seventeenth century it occurred to one man that people would be prepared to pay to be carried between Edinburgh and Leith.

Henric Andersen, from Stralsund in Pomerania, was granted a fifteen-year monopoly in 1610 to run passenger coaches between the city and the port. There is no record of his ever having managed to get the business going, and it is doubtful if anything at all happened, for he would have had to import the coaches — there being none in Scotland — and also the drivers. Two or three horses would be needed to pull a loaded carriage over the Easter Road, and that would require a skilful driver. The Restoration of the Monarchy in 1660 seems to have triggered off an outburst of enterprise, and in that year Adam Woodcock applied to the Town Council and was given leave to

South Leith Station: Dating from 1838, this is the oldest passenger railway station in Scotland.

carry passengers between Edinburgh and Leith for four pence per head. As he was also allowed to accept hires for anywhere outside Edinburgh, the coach run to Leith fell somewhat short of a regular service. Alexander Campbell, the Leith historian, remarked, 'In this state of matters, we may presume that the first inquiry would be, not ''When does the coach start for Leith?'' but ''Will there be a coach for Leith today?'' '

Woodcock's coach appears to have prospered no better than Andersen's, half a century earlier; but there was a growing conviction that there ought to be scope for a dependable service of transport to Leith, and a quick succession of optimists tried to make a success of the business. Tradesmen and merchants in the seventeenth century took a poor view of the idea of competition or rivalry. Far from increasing efficiency, it was considered that competition would have the opposite effect. Rivals would lower standards, take risks, resort to various malpractices for the sake of snatching business. The first requisite in starting a business was to secure a monopoly for a period, which would enable the new enterprise to become firmly established before any others appeared on the scene.

An Edinburgh merchant, William Home (or Hume) was granted a twelve-year monopoly in 1677 to operate a four-horse coach carrying ten passengers at 2s each in summer and 3s in winter. The service was to operate from 6 a.m. to 8 p.m. in summer and from 8 a.m. to 6 p.m. in winter, leaving from a stance at the foot of Leith Wynd. Again, however, there seem to have been snags, and Home soon sold the monopoly to Alexander Daes, who died in 1684. Although no one had thus far made a success of this public transport, there was no lack of applicants to take over after Daes' death, and in 1686 the magistrates decided to exercise some control over the business. Instructions were issued stipulating that coaches must be wind and rainproof and that each operator must supply ten cartloads of shingle or gravel for road maintenance. This last instruction represents all that was ever attempted to combat the rapid deterioration on the road. Regular users like the Carters and the coach operators were obliged to throw down gravel, which was a useless gesture, as, without any foundation to the road, the gravel speedily disappeared. As the eighteenth century progressed and traffic increased, the conditions on the roads became steadily worse.

Robert Miller ran coaches from 1702 to 1711, and during the time he was in business the Town Council made rules for coaches. They must not be driven by young boys. After dark a coach must have a light either carried in front, or secured to the box. And except by special licence coaches were forbidden on the Sabbath. The next man in the business, so far as records go, was John Balfour of Pilrig, who with some partners formed the Leith Coaching Company in 1722. This was a bigger enterprise than any that had gone before. On a feu just east of Timber Bush this firm had coach-houses, stables, and a hay-yard. Their coaches carried six passengers at 3d ($1\frac{1}{2}$p) each in summer and 4d (2p) in winter, but a disastrous fire destroyed their premises in 1727, and the partners announced they were giving up, as they had lost all their equipment. But the coach service was now considered essential, and public concern was such that subscriptions were called for and sufficient capital raised for the firm to make a fresh start. By July 1728 there were two coaches running, which provided an hourly service each way.

Despite the obvious need for public transport, despite the obvious public goodwill, Balfour's coach service did not last long. There were more difficulties than the state of the road, for the countryside around Edinburgh had become a favourite haunt of highwaymen, and the coach on the Easter Road was too easy a target to miss. The newspapers of the day printed accounts of these attacks on the slow, lumbering, defenceless coaches. Another attempt at a service was made by John Paxton in 1751. Paxton was innkeeper at the White Lion in the Canongate, and the coach he began running to Leith — there was just a single coach — had a white lion painted on each side of it. In time there were two coaches on the road again, but they were great, heavy springless vehicles with a coachman, a postilion and three horses which took an hour and a half to cover the mile and a half down to the Shore.

At the same time a much more efficient form of travel had long been available for those who could afford it. This was the hackney coach — the ancestor of the taxi. Hackney coaches also seem to have first taken to the roads in or about that same magical year of 1660, when the King began to enjoy his own again. In 1669 the Town Council ordered all hackneys to pay an annual fee of ten merks for the privilege of using the causey. Four years later hackneys were ordered to be numbered for identification, a list of owners was made, and fares were regulated. In 1765 David Gun, a hackney coachmaster, decided to challenge the stage coach to Leith by introducing two coaches to run at hourly intervals. He claimed he would cover the distance in fifteen minutes instead of more than an hour, which the stage coaches needed. And if the demand justified it, he would eventually provide a half-hourly service. Gun's coaches became known as the 'Leith Fly', but his was not a public service, for the Fly had to be hired. This was expensive, but offered great advantages. Hitherto a Leith merchant with business in Edinburgh had to spend over an hour in the coach journeying there. Arrived in the city, he could spend only a few minutes doing business if he wished to return by the same coach, or else he had to spend well over an hour in the city before catching the next coach for another long journey back. With the Leith Fly he was in Edinburgh in quarter of an hour, could spend three quarters of an hour there and then return by the same coach to Leith. The Fly carried four passengers and was drawn by two horses. It met with considerable success.

Public transport now began rapidly to improve. Two years after the introduction of Gun's Fly, coaches were running regularly between Edinburgh and Dalkeith, Musselburgh, Haddington, Stirling, Perth, Glasgow and London. The opening of the North Bridge in 1772 diverted some traffic from Easter Road to Leith Walk, and in that same year Parliament passed the Traffic Regulation (Scotland) Act, compelling every commercial vehicle to exhibit the name and address of the owner. It was forbidden for two vehicles to drive abreast and so obstruct the highway, and 'Drivers of loaded Horses &c., and Drivers of Carts, Coaches and Carriages, shall on meeting other Horses or Carriages, drive to the left hand or near side'.

The new route by Leith Walk was the shortest line from the city to the port, but it was desperately rough and rutted. At the foot of the Walk the track curved to the right to skirt the remains of the ancient town wall and the churchyard of South Leith. The ground was so rough here that coaches not infrequently overturned. Not surprisingly the journey still took about an hour and a half. This, to be sure, included a halt at the Halfway House — a tavern near the Gallowlee. This afforded the passengers some respite and refreshment, while the coachman mended harness and the horses had breathing space. A very popular and cheap drink at that period was shrub, and the large quantities consumed at the Halfway House by coach passengers no doubt got the place the name of Shrubhill. The Leith Police Commissioners ordered the area at the foot of the Walk to be causewayed in 1783, but it was only in 1793, when Constitution Street was driven through the churchyard down to Bernard Street, that an immense improvement in communication between the High Street and the Shore was established.

By the early years of the nineteenth century the public was better served by stage coaches than ever before. Two separate half-hourly services ran to Leith in 1806 — one from William Bell's, opposite the Tron Kirk, and the other from Porteous's at the head of Covenant Close. Another coach travelled from the city to Newhaven via Bonnington Bridge, making the journey there and back three times a day. The hackney coaches were also busy, charging half a crown ($12\frac{1}{2}$p) from the High Street to the Shore — for which journey the stage coach charged only sixpence ($2\frac{1}{2}$p). Hackney passengers also paid a 3d toll at the Pilrig toll-bar, although if they returned the same day they did not pay a second toll.

At that period there was no police force, and every individual had to protect his own property. Just after the end of the Napoleonic Wars, David Thorburn, a young divinity student in Leith, paid a visit to an uncle in London. He travelled by the London stage from Edinburgh, and found himself the only inside passenger at the start of the

'Dandy' car: When the North British Railway took over the Leith line in 1845, this was the type of passenger coach in use.

journey. The coach passed down Leith Street, along the London Road and Easter Road to Leith Links. Skirting the Links by Vanburgh Place and Hermitage Place, the coach reached the coast at Seafield, and thence it proceeded by Craigentinny Meadows — the Malaria Meadows, as this stretch was commonly known. A line of white painted posts indicated the firm ground through these swamps, and the route then became roughly the same as the modern A1 road. Well down into the Borders, on a very desolate stretch of the road, the driver suddenly bent down and shouted into the coach, 'Hide your money!' Thorburn, still alone, opened the windows on either side, drew out two pistols he carried, cocked them, and rested one on each window ledge. Presently galloping hoofs were heard approaching and two highwaymen appeared, one on either side of the coach; but apparently seeing the pistols, they did not linger, and galloped off again. This was the kind of incident any long-distance traveller had to anticipate in those days.

For longer journeys from Leith it was often more feasible, and certainly cheaper, to go by sea. Cabin fare from Leith to London was two guineas, and for steerage one guinea. Advertisements promised cabin passengers 'each a single bed, and the best of usage', but complaints about ill-usage and bad food multiplied. As roads improved, the shipping companies had to face increasing competition from stage coaches, and learned to pay more attention to the needs and comfort of passengers.

Traffic up and down and over the Forth between Leith and the many small towns and fishing villages was always brisk, and since there was no effective competition from the roads on these routes, the river trade was largely unorganised. The crossing to Kinghorn by ferry boat was in constant demand all the year round, weather permitting. By the mid-eighteenth century there were two types of craft on this run. The so-called 'Big boats' carried horses, cattle and other freight, as well as passengers; and the small pinnaces — some of no more than six or seven tons, carried passengers only. Until 1773 there seem to have been no regulations governing this service. The pinnaces were popular, as they were dependable, and charged only 6d (2½p) for the trip. In summer it was no uncommon thing for the Big boats to get the chance of a profitable cargo, which they would accept, departing then on a coastal trading trip that left the ferry service one boat short for the transport of heavy goods. On the other hand the pinnaces had the bad habit of taking on far more passengers than was safe. Pinnace owners answered this charge by alleging that the Big boats would not make the trip at all until they had loaded not only their freight, but also what the skipper decided were enough passengers. Undeniably there had been serious accidents with overcrowded pinnaces, but at the same time something would have to be done to compel the Big boats to be more dependable: so the Town Council issued regulations in 1773.

There were then eight Big boats and ten pinnaces engaged in the service, and one surprising fact was that the wages bill for the owner of a Big boat was not much more than that faced by the pinnace owner. The Big boat was manned by a crew of four men and a boy, and each pinnace, small as it was by comparison, still required four able-bodied men. This was necessary because, while the pinnace sailed well with a steady breeze, when there was little wind it had to be rowed to maintain the service. In calm weather the Big boats did not attempt the crossing, and while they remained in harbour waiting for a breeze, or hoping for a full load, the pinnacemen would approach the Big boats' prospective passengers, offering a quick and cheap passage. Often enough this manoeuvre ended in a fight between rival crews.

The regulations of 1773 laid down sailing times for Big boats, no

Leith tramcar: The earliest electric cars had no roof on the upper deck. This picture shows the later, improved version of the car.

matter how much cargo they might have, limited the freight charges to a maximum five shillings, and forbade overloading with passengers, especially in bad weather. Pinnaces were restricted to carrying a total of six passengers, and fares were ordered to be raised from 6d to 10d. These rules suited nobody; they were considered unfair and unworkable. Argument over the regulations became even fiercer when the carriers using the ferry joined in and addressed a petition to the Justices of the Peace. These packmen had been accustomed to cross on the pinnaces, but the new rules ordered that their packs should in future be counted as freight, only to be carried on the Big boats. The upshot of their petition does not appear, but evidently there was much in the ferry service that needed reform.

In contrast to the picture of inefficiency presented by the Forth ferries, the introduction of the sailing smack was universally considered to be a leap forward in maritime travel. Built mainly for the Leith to London run, and constructed on the 'cod head and mackerel tail' principle, the smacks earned a great reputation for speed. They measured up to 75 feet in length, with 25-ft beam, the greatest beam being more for'ard than aft, and their burden was up to 160 tons and more. One observer described them as having 'a tall thick mast with a heavy running-out bowsprit, and a very large mainsail'. Favoured by wind and weather, they were remarkably swift. One of them was reputed to have made the voyage from Leith to London in just over forty hours, which set the town talking for weeks. In adverse conditions, however, the smacks were poor performers, and very uncomfortable for the passengers. It was annoying, to say the least, to sail from London to the Forth in less than two days, only to be held for several days off the May Island and within sight of Leith, waiting for a favourable wind to make the harbour. When steamers began to make the same trip in the 1830s, they did no better than five knots, but they kept it up; they were dependable. The day of the smack was ended.

The first smacks were put on the London run in 1791 by the Leith and Berwick Shipping Co. who in that year moved their headquarters from Berwick to Leith. Like the stage coach they rapidly won popularity, but just as rapidly passed away. In barely half a century the stage coach was superseded by the railway; and the smacks, in an even shorter period, were eclipsed by the steamers. By the late 1830s the three companies which operated smacks had been given up. Over the years several companies had been involved, but unions and regroupings had left these three firms in command of the situation: these were the London and Leith Old Shipping Co., established in 1812 out of the former Leith and Berwick Co; the London and Edinburgh Shipping Co., which emerged in 1809, taking over the Edinburgh and Leith Co., dating from 1802; and thirdly, the London, Leith, Edinburgh and Glasgow Shipping Co. was born of a merger in 1820 between two smaller businesses.

The railway came to Leith in 1838, when a branch line from the Edinburgh and Dalkeith Railway (the 'Innocent' Railway) was led from Niddrie to Portobello, and through Craigentinny Meadows to Leith. The main purpose of this extension was to facilitate the transport of coal from the Lothian coalfield for export. The line ended at the foot of Constitution Street, and from there the coal was carted to the Shore. There were then no docks apart from the East and West Old Docks on the other side of the river. Ships and cargoes were very small, by later standards, and the railway line was laid for the use of trains consisting of a single coach, which was horse-drawn.

Until 1845 all the rail traffic to Leith was horse-drawn. South Leith station still survives as the oldest passenger station in Scotland, although passenger traffic ceased there when Leith Central station

Foot of the Walk c.1905: Showing the newly laid electric tram-lines.

was opened in 1903; and the old station buildings may not survive much longer if the site is redeveloped. The entrance to the booking-hall from the street, the station-master's flat and the short platform are still to be seen, as also the turntable used for locomotives after they came into use on this line. In those early years no tickets were issued. A Parliamentary inquiry was held in 1839 to discover the reason for this, and the manager of the line was examined. He said, 'Many people will not tell, or make up their minds, where they are going, which causes great confusion'. The North British Railway took over the Leith line in 1845, linking it with their line from Edinburgh to Berwick, which went by Portobello, and the line between Portobello and Niddrie was abandoned. Locomotives were now brought in to replace the horses, and a small station was built opposite the N.B.R. Portobello station. Here the line from Leith now ended, and the two stations at Portobello were linked by a subway. For half a century this five-minute run from Leith to Portobello was maintained, until the opening of Leith Central station made this little passenger route redundant.

143

The Leith and Portobello line was a happy-go-lucky Victorian institution. One authentic story illustrates this. A Leith merchant with business premises in Constitution Street had occasion to travel to Portobello twice weekly, and naturally used the convenient railway. As he lived near Seafield, he had an arrangement with the driver and guard that the train would slow down as it reached Seafield from Portobello in the evening, when the commuter would jump off, climb a wall, and be home in a few minutes. This arrangement worked smoothly until on one occasion the athletic businessman jumped from the train, fell, and broke his leg. This was doubly unfortunate, as he had no claim against the railway company in respect of his injury.

While the opening of Leith Central brought passenger transport from Leith to Portobello to an end, the little line remained an important route for goods traffic, and increasingly important as the century advanced. Before the start of the First World War an extensive upgrading of the line took place to cope with the ever-increasing output from the Lothian coalfield. New bulwarks were constructed along the Seafield beach to allow a double line to be laid, and a large area of the Craigentinny Meadows was levelled for the accommodation of sidings. This development transformed the appearance of the Seafield neighbourhood. The lush grass and the fine, clean, sandy beach were obliterated and are now forgotten.

The North British Railway extended into North Leith in 1849, when the Citadel Station was built; then in 1864 their great rivals the Caledonian Railway brought a goods line to Leith, and opened a passenger station at the west end of the docks in 1879. The two companies were in fierce competition, bought the land adjacent to their lines and built much tenement property there for their employees. The ordinary citizens, however, did not have to choose between one railway line and another, but between the railway and the omnibus.

When the first omnibus appeared in the summer of 1833 it was a great novelty, and the stage coach was quickly abandoned. Roads by then were far superior to what the eighteenth century had known, and the omnibus was welcomed for its speed, and moderate fares, which averaged a penny per mile. The first service in Leith ran from Edinburgh High Street to Seafield Baths. This new form of transport called for a new code of manners, and *The Scotsman* listed some basic rules:

Leith Harbour c.1895: Photo by John McKean, Ferry Road. McKean recorded many subjects in Leith towards the end of last century.

Being seated, keep your knees close together... If you don't you thereby occupy the space of two people...

Besides, it is a very unpicturesque attitude, and displays a susquepedality of paunch to great disadvantage.

Never stare the women out of countenance... If you must stare, stare at a man.

Don't intrude your talk upon those who don't want it...

Don't bring brown paper parcels with you into an omnibus — nor bundles of any sort. An omnibus is not a van.

Never turn up your nose at your fellow passengers; but whenever you feel your gorge rising at their humble condition, recollect that they pay the same fare as you do...

Don't spit upon the straw — and take care never to blow your nose with such energy as to startle your fellow travellers.

When you are about to alight, have your money ready in the exact coin; the conductor is not a banker, that he should give you change.

145

Not only had the exact fare to be tendered on these early omnibuses, but smoking inside was prohibited, and the conductor, if necessary with the assistance of the driver, was ordered to refuse to accept as passengers intoxicated or disorderly persons, and dogs. Under the circumstances there could be no precise timetable, but the journey from Edinburgh to Leith was expected to take anything from eighteen to twenty-five minutes.

In the 1830s and 1840s the omnibuses had no rival, for the old, clumsy stage coach was quickly out of fashion and the railway had not yet emerged with any real challenge as a means of passenger transport. The result was what might have been expected. The dashing new omnibuses, with their rules for passengers and comparative dependability, deteriorated from year to year until their condition became a public scandal. The buses were derided as rickety boneshakers, and in 1847 the *Leith Herald* commented: 'As might be expected, the animals which drag these machines can hardly be called horses; they are more like horse-frames, which by some internal mechanism are compelled to jerk themselves forward after a most unnatural fashion'.

All through the 1850s this state of affairs continued. Two operators supplied the omnibus service between Leith and Edinburgh. John Croall had a stage coach factory at Middlefield, where he now built omnibuses, and he had six of these on the Leith Walk run. David Carse & Co., coachbuilders at Orchardfield — that section of Leith Walk between the later Balfour Street and Springfield — ran four omnibuses over the same route. Their rivalry apparently did nothing for efficiency, as they were content to share a dependable market. At last, in 1861, William Lindsay, the Provost of Leith, decided to make a move in the public interest. In his professional life Lindsay maintained the unlikely occupations of solicitor and shipowner, and he was a shrewd, energetic and persistent man. He interviewed the two omnibus proprietors, pointed out the defects in the service, and asked for improvements. The omnibuses were too small and narrow, and as often as not badly overcrowded. Croall and Carse both promised to remedy what was wrong, but John Croall pointed out that, first, the buses conformed to the measurements laid down by Act of Parliament; and second, in regard to overcrowding, the introduction of the crinoline meant that ladies required more room than formerly. He also complained that the very bad state of the road not only shook the passengers severely, but very quickly ruined even

Railway Engine by Hawthorn of Leith: This shipbuilding and railway engineering yard was on the site later occupied by the Eldorado Stadium and the State cinema.

the most stoutly built omnibus. The Provost accepted this complaint and directed the town clerk to raise the matter with the City Paving Board.

The firm of Messrs. Dougal and Ritchie began running an omnibus in Leith in 1864, but Croall and Carse between them managed to make life so difficult for the newcomer that the bus was quickly withdrawn, leaving the two original operators a clear field again. But not for long. The first tramway went into service in November 1871 along the route from Haymarket by Princes Street and Leith Walk to Bernard Street; and just as the stage coach was superseded by the omnibus, so the latter had to give way to the tram, which provided a smoother, more comfortable ride. John Croall survived, however, supplying horses for the new trams, and before long he was also building tramway cars instead of omnibuses.

The horse tram improved the comfort of passengers, but the burden on the horses was no less severe. These cars were double-decked, had solid-rimmed wheels, and accommodated thirty-five to forty passengers. They were drawn by two horses, and the average life of a horse pulling a tramcar was four years. A large lamp at each end of the tramcar afforded light, when needed, and the conductor now issued tickets in the form of pieces of paper torn from a book where counterfoils were retained.

In little over twenty years the horse tram had fallen from favour, and in 1895 both Edinburgh and Leith were considering the advantages of adopting the cable-car system. Edinburgh decided in its favour and at once went ahead with the project before Leith had made up its mind. When Leith Town Council finally rejected the idea, Edinburgh had gone so far in committing money to the scheme that withdrawal was impossible, and so began an infuriating delay at Pilrig, when Leith passengers bound for Edinburgh had to change from horse-tram to cable-car. In 1905 Leith opted for the electric system, which was superior to the cable-car, but did nothing to end the muddle at Pilrig, which continued until after the amalgamation with Edinburgh, and the adoption of the electric system by the city in 1922.

CHAPTER 10

Church and Community

One vital element in the life of Leith for centuries was the involvement of the organised Church with the community. After the Reformation the kirk session of the parish church was responsible for poor relief, the care of the sick, and the education of the young. The elders were concerned with maintaining standards of behaviour, and in co-operation with the local bailies they dealt with petty crimes and misdemeanours. In the modern world most of these functions have been taken over by local and central government, and professionals have replaced the old-time amateurs. The kirk sessions fell far short of perfection. From time to time they showed themselves narrow-minded, and occasionally vindictive. On occasion they were obviously prejudiced, obtuse, and guilty of over-reaction to situations they thought presented danger. Often enough they were ignorant and suspicious, and made heavy going of many a simple issue. On the other hand these faults are common to all generations, and the same kind of accusations are mounted today against those in public office. It should be remembered that by and large the elders had the overwhelming support of public opinion. They had to face and try to cope with situations of desperate need with very limited resources. The kirk session, like the incorporations and the rest of the inhabitants, were gradually discovering how to live harmoniously in community. The community spirit develops through generations of living together, making mistakes, suffering the consequences, facing difficulties and frustrations and overcoming them, and from time to time throwing up outstanding characters. Throughout the kaleidoscopic experiences of the centuries the kirk sessions have been leaders and representatives of the people. The story of the Church in Leith is as varied and complicated as the story of the town itself.

In pre-Reformation times Leith was a village on the outskirts of the parish of Restalrig. The kirk at Restalrig was first erected at an unknown date, but in 1296 Adam of St. Edmunds, 'pastor of Restalric', swore fealty to Edward I. Whether the church had been planted there because of St. Triduana's well is not known, but the well attracted increasing numbers of pilgrims. Associated with the legend of St. Triduana, the water was reputed to benefit those with eye trouble. Restalrig attracted the attention of James III, who built a chapel royal there adjacent to the parish kirk — a notable hexagonal, two-storey structure where His Majesty endowed a chaplaincy in 1477. Ten years later the King erected the parish kirk into a college with a dean, and a programme of reconstruction and extension was initiated. This work does not seem to have progressed much after the king's death the following year, but James IV added six prebendaries to the establishment, and James V brought in singing boys. At the same time these three kings each made provision for the kirk at Restalrig with grants of land.

Within this parish, as already described, the Preceptory of St. Anthony was established in 1430, and a large Guild Kirk in 1483. In the mid-eighteenth century William Maitland, the Edinburgh historian, inspected South Leith Church and said it was plain that the building had been completed in stages — which is understandable. The Kirk of Our Lady in Leith, as it was known, was probably erected only as money and resources became available. First would be the high altar and the nave: later would come the great central tower, the aisles and the north and south transepts. It must have been an imposing place in the early sixteenth century. Both James III and James IV made donations to this New Kirk of Leith, but its time of glory was brief. In the English raids of 1544 and 1547 it appears to have had rough usage, was looted, and for a time served as a prison. George Wishart the reformer preached there in 1545, shortly before his martyrdom at St. Andrews. The final assault on the building came during the Siege of Leith in the spring of 1560. English artillery pounded the east end of the kirk to destruction. The chancel and transepts were destroyed, and the great tower collapsed. One chronicler recounts that on the morning of Easter Sunday that year, the service was proceeding despite the bombardment. As the priest celebrating Mass raised the Host, a cannonball crashed through the great east window — and that was doubtless the last celebration to take place in the original church.

Within a month of the death of Mary of Guise, the Queen Regent, and the accomplishment of the Reformation in Scotland, ministers were appointed to twelve of the principal towns in the land. David Lindsay, youngest of them all, was directed to Leith as the first Protestant minister of the parish. Lindsay was then nearly thirty years of age. He was a nephew of the Earl of Crawford, had newly

Paul preaching in Athens: Carved stone from the tympanum over the entrance to the former Kirkgate Church, Henderson Street, now on the wall of South Leith Parish Church hall.

returned from a sojourn in Europe, where he had acquired the new ideals and principles, and was already friendly with Knox and other reforming leaders. The first General Assembly of the Reformed Kirk met in December 1560, and one of its immediate decisions was to direct that the kirk at Restalrig be unroofed, and parish worship transferred to the semi-ruined building in Leith, which from then was to be the parish church. This change was only regularised by Act of Parliament of 1609, but from 1560 the parish church in fact was the nave of the Kirk of Our Lady in Leith.

Lindsay spent the rest of his life in Leith, dying there in 1613. That half-century was perhaps the most eventful in the history of Leith, for the port was near to the centre of government both of Church and State. The Reformation was a much more gradual affair than most of the histories would lead us to imagine. Decisions made by the Lords of the Congregation, by Parliament, Town Council or General Assembly were not always implemented as the decision-makers intended. Ideas and practices long entrenched in the daily lives of the people could not be swept aside for ever in the course of a few days or

F

months. The Preceptory of St. Anthony, partially ruined like the church, still continued active, despite the thundering denunciations of the old religion coming from the local authorities. Indeed when one of the brethren of St. Anthony's died in 1565, the vacancy was filled when James Tarbert was given a lifetime appointment; and Matthew Forrester, who became Preceptor in 1552, was still in office in 1567. While the old form of religion was proscribed, no one seems to have interfered with the canons at the Preceptory, whose services to the sick and aged had always been appreciated, and all of whom were known to many friends in the port. In course of time they simply grew old and died, and towards the end of the century the income from the wine tax was directed to the kirk session of the parish church on condition that the elders would use the fund for the same good work the brethren of St. Anthony had carried on. As a consequence the King James Hospital was built in the south-west corner of the churchyard, and here about a dozen old women were provided with bed, board and candle.

David Lindsay was on friendly terms with King James VI, who was said to prefer him before any other minister. Lindsay performed the marriage ceremony when the king was wed to Princess Anne of Denmark, and he baptised the royal children. He advised the king on many affairs and accompanied him to Whitehall in 1603. In the later sixteenth century the Kirk had not yet decided for Presbyterianism, and the ongoing debate between Presbyterian and Episcopalian ideas was often urgent and fierce. Lindsay leaned to the Episcopalian side, which endeared him to the King, but made him an object of suspicion to many in the Kirk. But the minister of Leith was a diplomat, with a gift for peace-making. This quality was widely recognised, so that time and again he was sent to different parts of Scotland where relations were difficult, to bring his calming influence to bear. This kind of work kept him away from his parish for months at a time. Several temporary appointments were made to supply the parish while the minister was on his travels, but eventually the incorporations in Leith made an agreement with the kirk session, that if a second charge were to be set up in South Leith, they would make themselves responsible for four-fifths of the stipend, if the session paid the remaining fifth. Presbytery agreed, and in 1593 a second charge was established.

By this time there were developments in North Leith. The chapel of St. Ninian had been taken down and rebuilt as a larger church, the

Interior of the Ukrainian Church, Dalmeny St: The several icons make a distinguishing feature of this church, unique in the city.

cost being shared among the inhabitants, and this new St. Ninian's was being served as a kind of mission station by a succession of ministers appointed there. The Presbytery now decided to erect this building into a parish kirk for that part of Leith 'benorth the brig'. The parish of North Leith was detached from the old lands of Holyroodhouse, and the thinly populated rural area was confirmed as the parish of North Leith by Act of Parliament in 1606. In South Leith, at the turn of the century, David Lindsay accepted nomination as Bishop of Ross, but he made no efffort to leave Leith, and at his death in 1613 he was still the parish minister of South Leith.

King James, like his Stewart successors,was obsessed with the idea of divine right and saw himself as the only true head of the Church.

To this idea Andrew Melville and all Presbyterians were implacably opposed, and so the struggle was joined which was to last for most of the seventeenth century. One development in North Leith took place peaceably, however: this was the addition of the lands of Hillhousefield and Newhaven to the parish of North Leith in 1630, the Newhaven area being detached from the parish of the West Kirk of Edinburgh — St. Cuthbert's.

The National Covenant of 1638 was enthusiastically signed in both South Leith and North Leith, by those minded to do so. But now party loyalties were becoming clear. The two ministers in South Leith at the time were both opposed to the Covenant. William Morton in the second charge quietly withdrew from his charge in 1638 without a word to anyone. William Wishart in the first charge was deposed in 1639 'for erroneous doctrine'. As he was reckoned to be 'a malicious railer against the Covenanters', he not only lost his charge, but was banished. The laird, on the other hand, John, 2nd Lord Balmerino, was one of the leaders of the Covenanting party, so in Leith it was difficult not to be involved on one side or the other in this dispute. While the English Civil War divided the country south of the Border, the Covenanting army were steadily recruiting in Scotland. General Leslie mustered the army on the Links, and when they marched south, the Rev. Alexander Gibson of the second charge in South Leith went with them as chaplain.

The martyrdom of King Charles shocked Scotland. It was one thing to oppose the king: to kill him was something quite different. The Covenanting army had to accept defeat at Dunbar, and Leith was occupied by the Ironsides, who took and used whatever they chose in the port. The troops camped on the Links, and the officers quartered themselves in private houses. Strict rules were laid down for the inhabitants which had to be obeyed. Soldiers took over Trinity House, the church, the King James Hospital and the Tolbooth — the only buildings of any account, where they lodged stores, equipment and weapons. The congregation had to worship on the Links at first, and then at Restalrig, in the old ruined church there. Eventually, when the Citadel was built and occupied as a garrison, the congregation was allowed to return to the church.

During the years of occupation the Cromwellian soldiers on the whole behaved rather well; a number of them married Leith girls, some even attended service in the kirk, and others, of the Baptist persuasion, organised worship in their own chapel at the Citadel.

South Leith Parish Church in the 18th century: At that period the roof completely obscured the line of clerestorey windows, which were only revealed at the rebuilding of the church in 1847. The churchyard was then rough and unkempt.

That was the first introduction of Baptist worship to Leith, but it faded again after the death of Cromwell and the departure of the English soldiery.

It was at this same period that Quakerism first took hold in the port: and the Quakers remained for a generation. Those were the 'Killing times' when Presbyterianism was out of favour, and those conducting or even attending conventicles were liable to arrest and heavy fines. Quakers, being against both Presbyterians and Episcopalians, found no favour in the community, and in 1676 Edinburgh Town Council ordered the suppression of Quakers in Leith, imposing a £50 fine for each meeting they held. The Quaker leader was a Leith skipper, Hector Allan, who not only had meetings in his own house during the time of service in the parish kirk, but at those meetings 'did vent many wicked and execrable tenets contrair to the principalls of the Christian religion'. Apart from his activities in Leith, Allan was also reported as having meetings at Prestonpans and Aberdeen — presumably ports where he docked his ship from time to time. Mr Allan finally overplayed his hand by interrupting the service in North Leith parish church one Sunday in 1678, and shouting to Mr Thomas Wilkie, the minister in the pulpit, 'Friend, I would know by what authority thou doeth these things'. He went on 'in several extravagant expressions to upbraid and scoffe' until a number of people in the congregation overpowered him and he was removed to prison — eventually to the Bass Rock. That was effectually the end of Quakerism in Leith.

Leith was not a zealous Covenanting area. The fanatical devotion to the Covenants found in Ayrshire and Galloway found small support in the seaport which time and again had suffered from the effects of religious quarrels pursued mainly by others. There were, however, some notable individual Covenanters. Thomas Stark, the miller at Leith Mills, was arrested in 1675 for accommodating a conventicle at his mill. The service was conducted by John Greig, 'ane indulged minister', who was in fact a brother-in-law of the miller, and other men arrested for attending the conventicle came from both Leith and Edinburgh. The magistrates were not hard on these prisoners. Various fines were imposed, and both Stark and Greig were sentenced to be imprisoned on the Bass Rock, but transport to the Bass was postponed, and eventually, after a few months in the Tolbooth, both men were released on appeal. Another arrest was made in 1681. This time the culprit was the Rev. William Wishart, an old man, who was fined £25 for conducting a conventicle in a private house in Leith, and lodged in the Tolbooth of Edinburgh. He, too, was leniently dealt with, as this had not been a field preaching, but a house meeting, early in the morning, before the hour of public service. So after two months in prison he was set at liberty, 'seeing he is ane aged infirme persone, brocken and disabled with many diseases. Not only the small remaines he has of health but his life also is in hazard, likeas his whole family is also under great sicknes and distresse'. The son of that 'aged infirme persone' became one of the most outstanding ministers of South Leith. Another notable Covenanter in Leith was the Master of the Grammar School, George Sinclair — perhaps the ablest of all the men who had the Grammar School in their charge. Sinclair refused to sign the Oath of Allegiance and lost his post at the school. He died in great poverty, but left an honoured name.

From 1660 the parish kirks in Leith were episcopal, until the Revolution Settlement in 1689 led to the establishment of

Detail from the hammerbeam roof in South Leith Church: This roof is said to have been copied from a church in St. Petersburg (Leningrad).

Presbyterianism. The argument had largely been about Church government rather than religious practices or the conduct of public worship, but there was a division in the congregations none the less, and when under the Indulgence of 1687 it was once more legal for Presbyterians to worship as they wished, there was an immediate breakaway from the parish church by those whose Presbyterian persuasion had not been weakened by thirty years of Episcopal rule. At first they met in a house they rented in Sheriff Brae, but this was soon found to be too small, so they removed to a new meeting-house built by Alexander Mathieson, one of the elders, and a wright to trade. Here they continued until 1693, when they transferred back to the parish church. The church building had been retained by the Episcopal section of the congregation under their minister Charles Kay, who showed remarkable ingenuity in finding ways to block the entry of the Presbyterians to the church which was now legally theirs. In August 1693 the Presbytery, with the Bailies of Leith, forced an entry to the church, changed the locks on the doors, and brought the Presbyterian congregation in, with their minister William Wishart.

The Episcopalians then presumably went to the vacated meeting-house in Mathieson's Wynd (later called Cables Wynd), but they did not remain there long, for their numbers dwindled. Most of them were Jacobite in sympathy, and Non-jurors — that is, they refused to swear allegiance to King William, and continued to pray for the exiled James Stewart. Their loyalty was admirable, but it set them on the wrong side of the law. Before long they were much reduced, and all their activities closely watched. It became illegal after 1707 for more than eight to worship in any house — eight, that is, not belonging to the family in the house. Their chapel in Yardheads was probably a room in Mr Kay's house. The '15 and '45 Rebellions made matters even worse for the Non-jurors, and after the '45 their meeting-house was shut up by order of the sheriff. In the meantime a 'qualified' congregation had emerged — that is, an Episcopalian congregation whose minister was prepared to pray for the lawful king and to swear allegiance to him. This was acceptable to the authorities. A local tradition claimed that there had been a 'qualified' congregation in Leith since the time of Queen Anne, but records of this congregation are extant only from 1749. From the start this was St. James's, and this choice of saint may have had reference to the exiled James many of them continued to regard as their rightful king. The Disabilities Act was repealed in 1792, allowing all Episcopalians freedom to worship, and this speedily brought together the two wings of the Episcopal Church in Leith. In 1805 they built themselves a church in Constitution Street and became one congregation.

The story of Presbyterianism in the eighteenth century is a dismal tale of argument and schism. The reintroduction of patronage in 1712 brought immediate discontent and eventual rebellion. Patronage was the system whereby a minister was chosen and presented to a vacant charge without reference to the congregation. The right of patronage was usually vested in the largest landowner in the parish, or in the Crown. In many cases vacancies were supplied

St. Ninian's Church: This was the parish church of North Leith before the present church in Madeira Street was opened in 1816. All that remains today is the curious little Dutch steeple from the 17th century.

with little or no trouble, as the patron consulted local feeling before making any choice. But there were many bitter controversies. A vacancy in the first charge at South Leith occurred in 1740, and the patron, Lord Balmerino, consulted with the kirk session before presenting William Aitken to the charge. The congregation were invited to vote for the presentee. The vote, of course, had no influence over the situation; it was merely an opportunity for the people to express their mind. As it happened, the majority of the congregation voting approved of the laird's choice; Mr Aitken was inducted and became a well-loved and able minister in the charge. But John Reid, assistant master in the Grammar School, objected to the principle of patronage, claimed that the congregation ought to have power to choose a minister for themselves, and in protest left the parish kirk and joined the Seceders, taking about forty followers with him.

The Secession Kirk had been formed in 1733 when four ministers had withdrawn themselves from the General Assembly in protest against the Patronage Act. John Reid and his followers now travelled to Bristo in Edinburgh each Sunday to worship with the Edinburgh Seceders under the Rev. Adam Gib. This arrangement continued for

159

twenty-five years until in 1765 they managed to set up as the Leith Antiburgher congregation, worshipping at first in the old meeting house in Cables Wynd, and then building themselves a church in the Carters' yard, adjoining South Leith churchyard on the north side. Here they remained and grew steadily, but became involved in more controversy. Their first minister, John Proudfoot, was deposed. He was a warmhearted, friendly man, but an alcoholic. Most of the congregation remained loyal to their disgraced minister, and with him they joined the tiny sect of 'Lifters'.

There is no space here to describe the many disagreements that divided the Secession Church. In 1747 an argument developed over the Burgess Oath, which was designed to exclude Roman Catholics from public office. Some Seceders scrupled to sign this oath, but others saw no harm in it. This produced the two sects of Burghers and Antiburghers. The Lifters were a small group who objected to Adam Gib's dictatorial ways as a leader in the Secession Kirk, and when Gib insisted that it was wrong to lift the bread and wine at communion when consecrating these elements, this little group tried to form their own sect. It was a short-lived movement, and John Proudfoot went over to them as they were the only part of the Secession Kirk who would have him after his deposition. A few months later Proudfoot died, and his followers sought entry to the Burgher communion, where they received a somewhat reluctant welcome.

The minority of the Antiburghers in Leith now formed their own congregation and built a church in St. Andrew Street, from which they transferred in 1826 to a larger building in St. Andrew's Place. By that time the old breach between Burghers and Antiburghers had been mended by a union in 1820, and both congregations were now part of the United Associate Church in Leith. A third United Associate congregation was also to be found in North Leith. They had branched off from the Kirkgate Burghers in 1816, and after a short spell in the vacated parish church of St. Ninian they had a church erected in Coburg Street. Another strand in the Secession movement was the Relief Church. Originating in the mid-eighteenth century, the Relief was a more moderate, open-minded kirk than the Burghers or Antiburghers. In 1822 a Relief congregation was founded in Leith, worshipping in old St. Ninian's, available again after the departure of the North Leith Burghers to Coburg Street. The Relief continued at St. Ninian's for almost three years, while

The 'Burning Bush': This stone graced the wall of the original North Leith Free Church at the corner of North Junction Street and Coburg Street. That congregation moved to Ferry Road in 1859, taking the stone with them.

Junction Road Church was being built for them on ground that had formed part of Bowershall nursery. In the somewhat narrow and bigoted air of Church life at that period the Relief Kirk was known for its broadmindedness, and Junction Road Kirk was considered 'a great kirk for captains and company porters'.

All that remains today of the old St. Ninian's Parish Church of North Leith is the quaint little Dutch steeple that adorned it. But it had been just a village kirk, and when the population rapidly increased with the upsurge of shipbuilding and related trades in North Leith, the old kirk was far too small to meet the needs of the place. A splendid new kirk was then built in Madeira Street and opened in 1816. By that time several other congregations of various persuasions were appearing in the port. In 1773 a group of elders in South Leith parish church, with their following, built a church on a piece of waste land that bordered the Links but was not part of that common ground. The site was an area of very rough ground where the remains of the old town wall were still encumbering the ground. This movement was the result of another contested settlement in a vacancy. This time the argument was over the choice of John Logan to fill the second charge. For the next half-century this new erection was known locally as the New Kirk, and it was peculiar in one respect. The office bearers in the new congregation claimed to adhere to the Church of Scotland so far as concerned doctrine, but they rejected presbyterian authority. Anxious to avoid another controversy, the South Leith kirk session acquiesced in the New Kirk's request for assistance in finding a minister. William Burnside was called to the charge in 1775, but he moved to Dumfries in 1780. The next minister was John (later Dr John) Colquhoun, who remained until he died in 1827. When the elders went to the presbytery after Dr Colquhoun's death, asking for a new minister, the presbytery insisted that the New Kirk must come under the authority of presbytery, or find a minister for themselves. The elders capitulated, so the New Kirk entered the Church of Scotland, and in 1834 it was erected into a *quoad sacra* parish church under the name of St. John's.

Restalrig Church had stood in ruins since the Reformation, but in 1837 it was roofed over again, made wind and watertight, and equipped for public worship. It then served as an out-station or chapel of ease for South Leith parish church. Three years later Sir John Gladstone of Fasque, a wealthy Liverpool corn merchant, who had been born and brought up in Leith, built and endowed a new parish church, with a manse, a school and an asylum for women with incurable disease. The new buildings included the site of the house where Sir John had been born. St. Thomas's Church was given a parish carved from South Leith parish, with the old St. Leonard's lands of North Leith parish.

Other denominations also appeared in the growing town. John Wesley paid several visits to Leith and made a deep impression. On one occasion he preached at the old meeting-house in Cables Wynd, popularly known as the Ark, or the Tabernacle. The crowd was so great that a window frame was removed, and Wesley stood on the sill addressing simultaneously the packed room within and the 'overflow' meeting outside. A Leith Methodist congregation was formed soon afterwards. Little is known of their early days, but a meeting-house of theirs in Coatfield Lane was in use in 1788. Then in 1815 they bought and fitted up a flat in Dock Street; and from there they moved to a much bigger chapel in Duke Street, on the site later to be occupied by Leith Central Station. Here they had room for 600 people, and this served them until they moved to their present location in Great Junction Street at the close of last century.

The Glassites also had a meeting-house in the later eighteenth century in Mason Lodge Court, off St. Andrew Street. This body, with their all-day Sunday services, which always included a 'love-feast', remained in the port for half a century, but faded from the scene in the 1820s.

The Congregationalists were much more firmly established. There is a tradition that the Congregational Church in Leith began as an open-air meeting on the Shore. This cannot be verified, but what is certain is that in 1805 forty-eight Leithers who had been attending the church of the brothers Haldane in the Tabernacle (on the site of the present Playhouse Theatre) formed themselves into a congregation and worshipped in a malt barn in Yardheads, which they had bought. When this accommodation became too small, they built a church in Constitution Street for about £2000 and moved there in 1826. (The site is now the north-east corner of Woolworth's block.) The other arm of Congregationalism came to Leith in the 1840s. Stemming from a series of revival meetings held in a room in the Signal Tower on the Shore in 1841, a move was made to a house in Morton's Entry in the Kirkgate in 1843, but it was soon necessary to find larger accommodation. The premises in Dock Street, where the Methodists had met from 1815, had been taken over as the Seamen's Academy, but the flat was now vacant, and it was here, on 19th November 1844, that the Second Congregational Church in Leith was formed. Three years later they bought the church in Storrie's Alley, off St. Andrew Street, where the Antiburghers had once worshipped. Here was set up the St. Andrew Street Chapel, which remained the home of the Evangelical Union Church until they finally moved to their Duke Street Church at the end of 1867.

The Evangelical Union congregation were succeeded in the Dock Street premises by the Baptists, who, it will be remembered, had made a brief appearance at the Citadel during the occupation by Commonwealth troops in the 1650s. The Baptist Union of Scotland sent James Blair, an evangelist, to rekindle Baptist fervour in the port in 1845, and they moved into the Dock Street flat when it became available. After a sojourn in a chapel at the foot of Leith Walk, an iron church was erected in Madeira Street in 1875, to be followed ten years later by the present stone building.

The Disruption of 1843 split the Established Church and added the Free Church witness to the religious life of the town. Just before the 1847 Union of the United Associate and Relief churches, there was another eruption in the Kirkgate United Associate congregation, who were then led by a reverend firebrand called William Marshall. Being deposed for various intemperate views and attitudes, Marshall induced the bulk of the congregation to follow him into a tiny sect known as the Calvinistic Secession Church. Like the Lifters of the eighteenth century, this body had only a brief existence, and Marshall demitted his charge in the Kirkgate congregation in April 1848. Then, with a group who still followed him, he took over an old wool store in Great Junction Street, fitted it as a church, and applied to be accepted as a congregation of the Original Secession Church. In the meantime the Union of 1847 had brought the United Presbyterian Church into being, and Marshall's old congregation in the Kirkgate were welcomed into that body, and in course of time became a vigorous congregation again. The Original Secession Church joined with the Free Church in 1852, so Marshall's new congregation in Junction Road became a Free Church congregation. William Marshall now fell into poor health. He travelled in the United States and Canada, hoping to benefit from travel. He returned to Leith only for a few months before receiving a call from his father's old congregation in Kirkintilloch, departing there in 1856. His church in Leith then became known as the Trinity Free Church, which had an unfortunate history. The former wool store where they were worshipping was found to be structurally unsafe, and the congregation built a new church in Hope Street, moving there in the summer of 1863. In December of that same year the new building was destroyed in a great gale. An old man recorded his memory of the scene when, as a boy, he joined the great crowd on the morning after the gale, viewing the stricken church, while the minister, the Rev. A. Stuart Muir, stalked about among the wreckage. Undeterred, the congregation at once set about building another church on the same site; but having built two new churches inside one year, they incurred massive debt. Trinity Free Church was finally defeated by this debt and dispersed. Their church was demolished to make way for a substantial new church built with funds

Scandinavian Lutheran Church: This little church in North Junction Street remains as a memorial to the days when Leith's trade with the Baltic countries created a large floating population of Scandinavian sailors in the port.

left by a Leith merchant, after whom this latest building was named the Elder Memorial. At the Union of the United Presbyterian and Free Churches in 1900 the Elder Memorial became a United Free Church. The Free Church minority who had opted not to join the Union now went to court and won a legal battle for repossession of various church buildings they had vacated at the Union. As a consequence the Elder Memorial reverted in 1907 to the Free Church.

The growing population was served by a proliferation of churches. U.P. congregations were started at Dalmeny Street, Bonnington and Wardie. St. Paul's, Lorne Street and the Abbey Church were parish churches with bounds drawn within the old parish of South Leith.

Restalrig Church was restored, extended and re-erected as a parish in 1912. Another chapel of ease from South Leith parish church was organised as the congregation of St. Mungo's in 1901, in a hall-church in Albion Road. This became a parish in 1923, but when the original hall-church was succeeded by a church in 1926, it was named the Lockhart Memorial, in memory of the fact that the church was built from a legacy made by the Rev. Dr. William Lockhart.

In 1848 the Roman Catholics bought Balmerino House in the Kirkgate and used the premises partly as a chapel, partly as a school, with a presbytery in Charlotte Street. Five years later their church, Our Lady Star of the Sea, was opened in the garden of the house.

A notable feature in the life around the docks was the large number of Scandinavian seamen to be found there. In 1864 a committee was formed with the cumbersome title 'The Scandinavian Seamen's Mission for Leith and Other Ports in the Firth of Forth', and the following year Andreas Michael Hansen was appointed as the first pastor to these seamen. Christian Salvesen and other Leith businessmen interested themselves in the mission, and in 1868 the Scandinavian Lutheran Church was opened in North Junction Street.

Another congregation somewhat out of the usual is the Ebenezer Church. Formed in 1891 from a group breaking away from Junction Road Church, they began worshipping in the Trafalgar Masonic Lodge in St. Anthony Place. This was a U.P. congregation, but their *raison d'être* was opposition to the use of alcohol in communion wine. In this sense they could be regarded as a branch of the temperance movement, and Ebenezer soon attracted members from other congregations in the town. The new congregation did not long remain without a church, for they soon bought the Junction Street Hall, which had served as a theatre and music hall, refurbished it and opened it for worship on 5th December 1895. *Leith Burghs Pilot* commented that the former music hall had an aspect of 'old, cold, uncharitable and forbidding bareness', which seems an odd description of a place of entertainment. However, 'the gallery has been run all round, and the antiquated and ungainly platform been supplemented by an elegant pulpit, behind which has been erected a pretty little organ'. Ebenezer, at any rate, were happy in the Great Junction Street Church until redevelopment of the area in the 1970s deprived them of it; but they are now happily ensconced in a modern church in Bangor Road.

Rev. David Kilpatrick: Minister of Newhaven Free Church, 1879-1917. He was a noted educationist, and the Junior Secondary School built in 1913 was named after him.

The kaleidoscopic picture of churches in Leith also included a variety of missions. Practically every congregation in the town sought to prove its vigour by conducting a mission in connection with the congregation. The mission halls were for the poorer people who could not dress respectably enough to go to church. Mission services were conducted by ladies and gentlemen from the congregations who regarded this activity as evangelistic work. Tea and buns and redemption hymns were all part of the mission service. In 1856 the Rev. William McKenzie of the North Leith Free Church approached the Town Council with a proposal to buy or feu the site of the former Laigh Fleshmarket in St. Andrew Street, to build a church for the poor. The scheme came to nothing, but the Victorian idea that this kind of apartheid within the Church was desirable or necessary is worth recording.

Primitive Methodism came to Leith in 1867, and for forty years this small group do not seem to have had any settled place of worship, but in 1907 they built their chapel at the corner of Easter Road and St. Clair Street and were active there for many years. The latest arrival has been that of the Ukrainians, who took over the former Dalmeny Street Church after the union between that congregation and Pilrig Church. Orthodox worship began there on 15th August 1965.

Apart from the Christian Church, the port of Leith has since the last war been the favoured location for most of the Sikh community in the city. When St. Thomas's Church fell vacant after the union of that congregation with the congregation of Junction Road Church in 1975, the Sikhs purchased the church and halls, and there they have their temple. The hall premises they have used for the development of their own social and community life.

CHAPTER 11

The Independent Burgh of Leith

In the summer of 1833 the reformed Parliament at Westminister passed an act providing that:

> from and after the first Tuesday in November next there shall be in each of the several Burghs and Towns of Paisley, Greenock, Leith and Kilmarnock, the Number of Sixteen Councillors, whereof one shall be Provost, four shall be Bailies and one a Treasurer.

This was the Act which established Leith as an independent burgh; and so were fulfilled the aspirations of Leithers for almost three centuries, during which the port had suffered what she considered to be persecution from Edinburgh. From the late sixteenth century the city had owned almost all the land on which Leith stood, and as feudal superiors had borne down hard on Leith in ways which were within the law, but which embittered relationships between city and port. From the mid-eighteenth century Leith had rapidly become industrialised, and increasingly restive under the mismanagement of Edinburgh. The causes of complaint were many and complicated, but the Act of 1833 was hailed as opening the door to emancipation and independence.

There was great excitement at the imminent prospect of independence. There had been a memorable procession of Edinburgh and Leith trades the previous August, in celebration of the passing of the Reform Bill. In August 1833 the Leith Trades, anticipating the even greater prize of independence now almost within their grasp, mounted another 'Jubilee Procession', in commemoration of the previous year's procession. The *Edinburgh Evening Courant* reported:

> Tuesday, a procession of the Trades took place at Leith, in commemoration of the Jubilee procession of last year, on the occasion of the passing of the Reform Bill. They assembled on the Links, between 11 and 12 o'clock forenoon, and after being marshalled, proceeded through the various streets of the town, up Leith Walk to the Toll-house, round which they marched, and returned to Leith Links, where they assembled round a temporary hustings erected in front of the High School, and were addressed by several gentlemen...

169

Before dispersing, a hogshead of porter was brought from the cellars of Captain Carnegie, and distributed among the tradesmen. The best order was preserved throughout the whole day.

The joy, however, was shortlived. It was soon apparent that the town council of Leith had immense problems. These had been there for long enough, but until now the onus of dealing with them had rested on Edinburgh. It had become an ingrained habit in Leith to blame Edinburgh for everything that was wrong; and indeed most of the criticism of the city's ignorance and ineptitude in dealing with matters affecting the port had been justified; but now that they were on their own, Leithers found the perspective had altered. The motto chosen for the new burgh was 'Persevere' — an apt reference to three centuries of persistent effort that had gone into achieving independence. Perseverance was going to be a virtue very much needed by the new town councillors.

One problem demanding an immediate answer was a dilemma in which Edinburgh had never been placed. The new burgh had no income. This incredible fact had arisen from an oversight in Parliament when the Act was passed establishing the burgh. The same Act erected Paisley, Greenock and Kilmarnock into burghs, and Parliament presumed that each new burgh would set up its own Common Good fund, which was the normal source of day-to-day income for a burgh. The Common Good drew from various sources, but chiefly from the imposition of small charges on goods known as petty customs. The legislators had overlooked the peculiar situation at Leith, where for centuries the petty customs had been delivered into the Edinburgh coffers. The city, of course, had been responsible for the cost of maintaining Leith. Much of the resentment and bad feeling between the capital and the seaport was latterly due to the fact that Edinburgh did not spend on Leith anything like the money she uplifted there.

Leith Town Council naively assumed that under the new Act Edinburgh would transfer the petty customs to Leith, but when the town clerk of Leith applied to have the necessary legal transfer put into effect, Edinburgh blandly answered that there was no mention of this in the Act, and that accordingly no transfer would take place! This piece of barefaced impudence was further complicated for Leith by the fact that within months of the port's independence Edinburgh was declared bankrupt. Municipal mismanagement had affected her own finances as well as those of Leith. The Leith town clerk was

Adam White, the first Provost: A merchant and business man with many interests, wealthy and influential, Adam White was an excellent choice for Provost in the early days of independence.

therefore advised that he would have to apply, not to Edinburgh, but to Edinburgh's creditors, for the right to collect petty customs. It soon appeared that the creditors were not disposed to let anything go that might bring them in even a small return. Not only that, but these gentlemen now actually began legal proceedings to secure for themselves the petty customs of Leith! Fortunately Mr John A. Murray, M.P. for the newly created Leith District of Burghs, was also the Lord Advocate. Leith Town Council asked him to try to get

The last Town Council: The families of several of these councillors are still active in Leith today.

an amending Act through Parliament quickly, to rectify the position of the new burgh. Mr Murray asked them to be patient, as he would prefer to introduce a Bill to cover all the Scottish burghs, so as to secure their financial rights. Leith accepted this proposal rather reluctantly, for that Bill would take much longer to prepare. In the event it was 1838 before the City Agreement Act was passed, giving Leith the right to levy petty customs, and so begin to enjoy a modest income.

It is important to remember these facts, because the stringent financial situation of the 1830s affected the council's judgement on many matters during the years to come. For the first five years of its independent life the Burgh of Leith had to live on credit. There was no money for necessary running expenses. The port was saved from bankruptcy by the fact that the councillors were mostly prosperous businessmen and merchants with many contacts. Money on loan came from several councillors and many townsfolk. This was enough to see the town through until 1838, when the City Agreement Act made it possible to set up a Common Good fund; but by then there were massive debts to numerous people, and all through the 1840s the council continued to be very short of money, as some creditors began pressing for the return of their loans. Matters improved, but the tight-fisted, parsimonious attitude of the Town Council throughout

John Lindsay, the last Provost: An able and hard-working Provost, it was his unenviable task to preside over the last years of Leith's independence.

most of its eighty-seven years of existence must have derived, at least in part, from those first years of independence.

Oddly enough it was not until the Third Police Act of 1827 that the boundaries of Leith were defined. Before then, even the magistrates did not know the limits of their own jurisdiction. Under that Act Leith was held to extend between Seafield toll-bar on the east, the Firth of Forth on the north, the stone bridge at Leith Mills on the west (that is Junction Bridge), and the foot of Leith Walk on the south. These limits excluded North Leith, and the whole of Leith Walk and the neighbouring lands. With the reform of Parliament, Leith, together with Portobello and Musselburgh, became a Parliamentary constituency known as the Leith District of Burghs, and the boundaries of the port were redefined. Leith then included the area between a line from Lochend to the sea on the east; low water mark

Burgh Chambers: Burgh Chamber, Police station and Courthouse were under the same roof. As the tower was only added to St. John's Church in the 1830s, all that can be seen in this picture is the entrance to the forecourt of the church.

on the Firth of Forth on the north; Wardie burn on the west; and the middle of Leith Walk (that is Pilrig) on the south. This was the territory to be administered by the new Town Council. There were then, by the 1831 census, 25,855 inhabitants. The population had grown from just over 15,000 at the beginning of the century, and it was still increasing steadily.

Crowded wharfs and congested streets around the Shore gave an impression of prosperity, but this was deceptive. Since 1760 the volume of trade at Leith had risen tenfold — from 34,000 tons to 340,000 tons in 1834; but foreign trade, always a small proportion of the total, had fallen from 17% in 1815, at the close of the French War, to 13% in 1834. The long war with France, in fact, had been good for Leith, for it was from Leith, alone among the Scottish ports, that convoys had set out for foreign ports, and so all the merchants in Scotland had virtually been compelled to channel their foreign business through Leith. That advantage disappeared almost overnight with the coming of peace. Since then Leith's coastal trade had been badly affected by the opening of the Union Canal in 1822, which siphoned away much trade with the West of Scotland. The opening of the Edinburgh and Dalkeith Railway in 1831 was a blow to the coal trade, which had hitherto been almost all seaborne through Leith.

During the previous three-quarters of a century Leith had been growing so rapidly, both in industry and in population, that it would have taken a very lively and able local government to cope with the inevitable problems accompanying such growth. And the port had had to suffer a local authority uninterested in its welfare, and quite ignorant of how to approach the problems of life in Leith. Since 1771 the Police Commissioners had been striving against great odds to provide water, sanitation and lighting for the town, as well as watching and warding the streets. There had been some progress, but the port still had a bad name. Adverting to William Chambers again, he remarked in 1832:

> The town of Leith is ... disagreeable from the filthiness of its streets. A person in proceeding out of the boundaries of Edinburgh into those of the seaport will perceive an immediate change in the appearance of the streets. Such an evil may perhaps be chiefly attributed to a laxity in the discipline of the police, and partly to the trading character of the town.

This criticism came rather oddly from an inhabitant of the city which had found it necessary to coin the warning shout of 'Gardyloo'. Leith was improving too. In 1822 a start was made with lighting the streets by gas, and in 1833 a prototype of the gas cooker was exhibited at the Mechanics' Institute. The first omnibus started to run between Edinburgh High Street and Seafield in the year Leith became independent, and a Prospectus and Plan of a railway to run between Edinburgh and Leith was published, although that particular line was never built. These were signs of progress.

Personal attitudes and habits did not change so rapidly. In 1833 a man seventy-five years old had been born in the Leith that was still a village. In the course of his lifetime that village had become a town, but the people still to a large extent preserved village attitudes. A letter to the *Edinburgh Courant* in 1828 makes this point:

> I have been surprised at the absurd practice, which is too common here, of walking upon the causeway, which, you know, is specially provided for horses and carriages. If you are riding or driving, these good people never think of getting out of the way, but look at you as if you were interfering with their rights in pursuing your ordinary course ...

William Marshall, in his economic review of Leith, constantly reverted to the theme of the necessity of Leithers modernising their ideas. Even the shipowners seemed quite unaware that the business world had been experiencing a revolution. He wrote:

> Every little consideration in the way of accommodation, despatch and economy, is now marked and taken into account ... Thirty years ago, half a dozen of successful voyages to the Baltic would have cleared the value of the ship, and laid the foundation of a competency for life. Such a thing can seldom be accomplished now ... There is now introduced into business a mode of calculation which, for strictness, was formerly unknown ...

Those who were living in the past must change their attitude and methods, or go under.

According to Marshall, Leith's trade was not suffering from exorbitant port charges. Charges were just as heavy at other ports. The trouble at Leith was an antiquated system of applying these charges. A ship using the harbour regularly throughout the year was only charged for eight voyages in twelve months, even though she might be making a weekly call at Leith. Foreign ships, however, had to pay every time they returned to Leith. Again, a hogshead of whisky was charged the same as a hogshead of ale; a ton of rags rated the same as a ton of tobacco or a tun of wine. This was the logic of bedlam, and urgently called for reform.

There were other anomalies. Leith had practically no Mediterranean trade, while Glasgow did a great deal of business there. On the other hand Leith imported more sugar from Mauritius than all the Clyde ports put together. Port charges notwithstanding, Leith had a far greater share of the wine trade than went to Glasgow. Even so, this trade was operated in a stupid way. Wine ships were tramps; they picked up various cargoes in a succession of ports, and wine was only part of their load. The wine was often of the highest quality, but spent far too long at sea. It was high time importers got together and chartered vessels for wine shipment alone.

Leith had a longstanding reputation as a fruit-importing centre, but in the 1830s almost all the fruit coming into Leith was brought there from London, instead of being shipped direct from Spain or Portugal. The reason for this peculiar arrangement was that fruit brought to London and transhipped there for Leith reached Leith two or three weeks earlier than it did when shipped direct from abroad in Leith vessels. This, in turn, was because the ships used in the fruit trade were invariably the oldest, clumsiest, heaviest, slowest ships afloat. It was madness to treat perishable goods in this way, but owners were reluctant to invest in new bottoms.

These were matters that concerned the Dock Commission, and the Town Council fretted and fumed at the lack of initiative in that quarter — especially as a pier at Granton was under construction, and a Bill was before Parliament to make a harbour at Trinity. Both Granton and Trinity could provide the deepwater facilities lacking at Leith. In June 1837 the Town Council petitioned the Government to take over the management of the docks and harbour — to nationalise them, in fact. They argued that the experiment of having a Dock Commission had failed. Leith had no accommodation for steamships, and the town had no money to invest in improving port facilities: nor were Edinburgh's creditors interested in spending money on the port. The petition was refused, but the make-up of the Dock Commission was revised.

While the general trade of the port was at a low ebb, the shipbuilding yards were active. In 1838 Robert Menzies & Sons built the *Sirius* of 450 tons with a 270 h.p. engine, and this was the first steamship to cross the Atlantic. Two years later the same firm launched the *Forth* for the West India Steam Packet Co., and for this launch part of the dock wall had to be removed to let this large vessel into the river. When Hugh Morton & Co. built the *S.S. Leith* in 1862 for Mr D.R. Macgregor, this vessel, at 1300 tons, was the largest ever to be registered at Leith up to that time. By the 1860s it was generally agreed that wooden ships had had their day, and it was remarked that a wooden ship had been on the stocks of one Leith yard for several years, having failed to find a purchaser. The practice then was for ships to be laid down as a speculation by the builder. Prospective buyers would stroll through the yards looking at what was on offer, and would agree to take a vessel that was half-built. The customer's own specifications could then be embodied in the finished craft.

The 1840s saw the adoption of steel in shipbuilding, and the Clyde yards, with coal and iron ore nearby, advanced rapidly. Only the smaller class of vessel could be built at Leith, and it was only in the later nineteenth century that the Leith yards learned the arts of specialisation, which brought them prosperity.

A thriving port meant a thriving town, and the course of the nineteenth century saw vast changes in the appearance of Leith. In the 1830s not much had changed from the eighteenth century. Shops such as the modern world takes for granted did not yet exist; there were no window displays or packaged goods. Fish and meat were sold in the markets; fruit and vegetables were to be had at several market gardens in the vicinity, or from carts in the street. Grocers sold their wares from bins or sacks. Tradesmen worked from rooms in their own homes, or in adjacent yards. Sanitation was minimal, and confined to the main streets. The 1845 Directory lists twenty-three cowfeeders or dairymen in Leith, and poultry still abounded. In 1839 some mischievous boys goaded horses grazing on the Links, and there was a wild stampede, to the public danger. From that date horses at grass on the Links were prohibited.

At that period there was little speculative building of houses, although a number of large villas were erected around the Links and at Trinity. When dock construction began in the late 1840s, and work on extending the piers went ahead, there was a large influx of Irish labour — part of the massive exodus from Ireland following the potato famine. Many of these navvies found work in Leith, not only in the docks, but also on the extension of the railways around Leith and Edinburgh.

The developing port was now attracting many people from the country looking for work, and a new class of white-collar worker began to emerge. Expanding business required more clerical staff from junior clerk to manager. Wine merchants, corn merchants, shipping agents, insurance brokers, banks, wholesale provision merchants and firms engaged in transport and distribution of goods were employing more people. The ranks of municipal employees were extending in all departments. This new class was important for the economy of the town, for their employment was assured all the year round. Winter frosts did not throw them out of work, and the demand for their services was constant. Their wages were modest, but since work was assured they could plan ahead and even save, as the labourer could never do.

From around 1860 a long programme of housebuilding got under way. This was speculative building; the Town Council did not intervene in any way to direct or plan this development. To meet the clamant need arising from gross overcrowding, ground was feued from the Pilrig estate, and the area south of Great Junction Street was rapidly occupied by Bonnington Road, Tennant Street, Burlington Street and other adjacent streets. These tenements met the demand for workers' housing, but they had no piped water above the ground floor, as the water company could not provide sufficient pressure to carry water upstairs. It was only in 1869, when the Leith and Edinburgh Water Companies at last amalgamated, that it was possible to take water pipes to the top floor, and of course this amenity carried with it an increase in rent. Not surprisingly there was no demand from tenants for hot-water pipes; cold water in pipes was a sufficient luxury. The extra plumbing for hot water would have raised the rents once more. Not all of the early tenement buildings were improved with extra plumbing after they were erected. In the 1890s the Superintendent of Police reported to the Town Council on the state of tenements in Fox Street and Poplar Lane:

> Neither tenement has any W.C.: each is four storeys high, and the only way the tenants have of disposing of their night-soil is by putting it into the grating on the street at the foot of the stair, or in the case of Poplar Lane, about thirty yards from the stair foot.

The next phase of housebuilding came in the late 1860s, when the Edinburgh Co-operative Building Society put up the rows of little houses with gardens between Lochend and Restalrig Roads. Mention has already been made of these, which were the first new houses to benefit from the improved pressure of piped water, and were in all respects more attractive homes than those tenements hurriedly run up for the workers. The trend towards better-class flats and terraced villas continued through the later years of the century, as Easter Road, Leith Walk and Ferry Road each acquired new tenement blocks — substantially built, well-proportioned flats for a higher class of worker. Cambridge Avenue and Gardens, and the Cornhill, Ryehill and Restalrig Terrace houses reflected the steadily rising standards of the period.

In the meantime the rows of two and three-storey tenements which had provided for the needs of the early days of the Industrial Revolution in Leith were in a dreadful state, grossly overcrowded and without sanitation. Under the Artisans and Labourers Dwellings Act of 1868 the Town Council undertook the first slum clearance scheme they had ever embarked upon. Provost Watt ordered the sanitary inspector to report on the slums of Leith, and as a result the great Leith Improvement Scheme was put in hand. The slums had to be cleared, but it is unfortunate that many picturesque street names were also lost. Sheephead Wynd, Darling's Brae, Vinegar Close, Peat Neuk, Tod's Hole Close, St. Leonard's Lane, Green Jenny

Lane were names that each pointed to some piece of history or legend. They all disappeared in the cause of town improvement, and modern names never seem to be so evocative.

Not only did builders have freedom to erect blocks of houses wherever they could secure a feu, but they also named these tenements and terraces according to their fancy. This has produced the paradox of a number of street names in Leith affording a perpetual memorial to the otherwise anonymous wives and daughters of various builders and landowners. Janefield, Jessfield, Elizafield and Annfield all refer to ladies who were no doubt charming, but who have left us nothing but their names. One or two gentlemen have also had their anonymity celebrated in John's Place, James Place and Allanfield. This practice of street-naming according to passing fancy had got out of hand by the 1870s, when Leith Walk, for example, had a different name every hundred yards or so, as Whitfield Place, Cassels Place, Queen's Place, Orchardfield, Springfield, Albert Place, George Place and so on — a postman's nightmare. In 1874 the Town Council ordered this practice to stop, so that one street should have but one name; but some of the old names lingered.

Along with slum clearance, ideas of the value of fresh air and exercise began to influence the magistrates, and towards the end of the nineteenth century concern was expressed that the town should acquire parks and open spaces for recreation. This was the thought behind the levelling of the Links as part of the Improvement Scheme in the 1880s. Within a few years other parks were negotiated for, and an agreement with the family of Balfour-Melville at Pilrig House resulted in most of what remained of the estate becoming Pilrig Park. Bailie Keddie presented two acres of ground on the north bank of the Water of Leith, which became rather a secluded little park off Ferry Road; and the grounds of Bonnington Park, home of Richard Raimes of Raimes Clark the manufacturing chemists, became Victoria Park, although popularly known for many years as Raimes Park. Starbank House, Newhaven was purchased by the Town Council, and the grounds were landscaped to form Starbank Park. In 1907 South Leith Poorhouse removed to Seafield, and the old building was demolished. The Hospital managers bought the site to secure more light and air around the hospital, and this was made available to the public as Taylor Gardens. In that same year the Town Council acquired land at Craigentinny and invited Ben Sayers, one of the great golfing exponents of the day, to lay out a nine-hole course there. Golf on Leith Links was then prohibited, and the Craigentinny course was extended to eighteen holes after the 1914–18 war.

In the early years of this century Leith was a seaport with some 75,000 inhabitants, increasing year by year. Local society comprised a great range of people, from the wealthy business and professional class, through the ranks of management and white-collar workers, down to a very large and very poor industrial proletariat. Poverty and disease presented apparently insoluble problems. Unemployment greatly increased in the winter months, and in a close-knit community such as Leith there was much concern as to how the hardships of poverty might be ameliorated. Dr Mitchell of South Leith Parish Church, with a team of ladies, organised a soup kitchen in January 1872, and thereafter this became an annual institution, serving many thousands of meals through the worst of the winter weather. About the same time the Society for the Improvement of the Condition of the Poor in Leith opened a House of Call for working men in Parliament Street. This was one of the first model lodging houses in the country, and it flourished and extended over the years, providing a home for men — especially single working men — at a very cheap rate.

An enquiry carried out in 1906 by Leith School Board (part of a national enquiry) found that many children in Leith schools were starving — not just malnourished, but starving. Official reports are not given to using emotional language, but certain vivid sentences light up the scene for us. In Leith schools there were 344 starving children. The Report commented:

> We are convinced that the attempt to teach the starving boys and girls who are found in the schools is utterly futile, and amounts almost to cruelty. In their case, education becomes little better than a farce.

It was as a direct result of this Report that free school meals were instituted. This was the condition of the families of the labouring population when there were no sickness benefits, unemployment relief or old age pensions.

There were also some wealthy people in Leith — shipowners, merchants, large employers of labour — and there were kindly disposed men among them, some of them personally extremely generous: but they could not transform the state of society. The outbreak of war in 1914 solved the problem of unemployment for the time being, but the end of the war brought to crisis point a situation that ought to have been faced a generation earlier, but which had been resolutely ignored by all those whose decisions mattered. By 1919 Leith had no viable future as a separate and independent community.

The difficulty in Leith was that sense and sentiment were closely intermingled. It was virtually impossible for any Leither to view the scene objectively, and for the mass of the people there was no immediate call to be objective. The man in the street was ignorant of the facts that mattered. On the other hand it had long been obvious to businessmen in the port that sooner or later there would have to be changes in the relationship between the city and the port. As scarcely a mile and a quarter separated Edinburgh G.P.O. from the Foot of Leith Walk, it made economic common sense that the public services of the neighbouring communities should be amalgamated. Moves had already been made in that direction. The merging of the two Water Companies in 1869 had been an unmixed benefit to Leith. The Gas Companies had also joined forces successfully. Difficulties had arisen over public transport, as Edinburgh wished to own the complete system. Leith would have agreed to a partnership — an eventual amalgamation perhaps — but certainly not a takeover. So the matter rested; but there were other services such as street cleansing and lighting, the Police and the Fire Brigades, that could certainly function better under an overall direction.

These facts were obvious, but any action would depend on a lead from the Town Council, and businessmen who were councillors did not bring the same arguments to council affairs that they used in conducting their businesses. No one suggested there was any urgency to make decisions everyone knew would have to be made at some future time.

Matters had been brought to a head in September 1894 when the town clerk of Leith received a letter from the town clerk of Edinburgh. Enclosed with the letter was a Memorandum and Outline of a Scheme of Amalgamation of Edinburgh, Leith, Portobello and the immediate areas; and the letter suggested a conference between the interested parties. One may imagine the shocked silence in the Council Chamber when this communication was read. Fortunately someone remembered the annual municipal election was due in about six weeks' time, so it was agreed to let the letter lie on the table until a freshly elected council could deal with it. Every councillor realised

Foot of the Walk: This was the scene in the 1890s when the possibility of amalgamation with Edinburgh was first suggested.

that anyone known to favour such a conference would certainly lose his seat at the forthcoming election. Yet three councillors courageously voted against that delaying move, and would have been willing to discuss the matter with Edinburgh.

With the Press present at the council meeting the matter could not be hushed up, and a public meeting was called in the Duke Street Hall. Out of the three hundred people who attended, only ten were prepared to have the proposal discussed with Edinburgh. In trying to shelve the matter the councillors at least were well aware of public opinion. Edinburgh in 1894 appears to have been quite unaware of the strength of feeling north of Pilrig over any suggestion of becoming entangled with the city again. Middle-aged folk had heard from their parents of the dreadful predicament of Leith before 1833. They had grown up hearing many stories of the mismanagement, chicanery and indifference to their needs that Leithers had suffered from their feudal superiors. Anything would be preferable to a new tie-up with Edinburgh.

At the same time those in public positions in Leith must have had their doubts. Since Leith had become independent, Edinburgh had several times obtained parliamentary acts to extend her boundaries.

Extensions to the city had taken place in 1856, 1882, 1885 and 1890; and it looked as though this trend would continue. The city, like the port, was growing; the demand for more housing made extensions inevitable. Leith had the same needs. In the 1890s the population was growing at the rate of about 1000 every year. Yet Leith Town Council had never made any attempt to extend the bounds of the port. Edinburgh extended again in 1896, taking in Portobello, and yet again in 1900; and in the following year the capital city bought up all the land adjacent to Leith both to the east and to the west.

The port was now in a serious predicament. There was extensive overcrowding in slum conditions, and an urgent need for expansion, but there was no room left to build any houses within the bounds. The councillors must have been well aware of this problem from the beginning of the century, but nothing was ever said in public, and the ordinary Leither had no inkling of the real situation. The Great War of 1914–18 shelved the issue, but by 1918 the plight of Leith was even more desperate as returning ex-servicemen added the problem of unemployment to the housing shortage.

In 1919 it became known that Edinburgh was seeking another Boundaries Extension Act, and this time Leith was to be engulfed. There was no lack of shocked and angry comment in the town, but true to form the Town Council did nothing while summer and autumn passed and the year drew to a close. With the New Year a lead came from the *Leith Observer*, proposing in an editorial that a plebiscite of the townspeople would settle the matter effectively. The assumption was that a definite refusal to amalgamate coming from the people would be an unanswerable argument. This galvanised the Town Council. A meeting was held on Thursday 15th January 1920 at which it was decided to adopt the suggestion of a plebiscite.

Time was running out; the deadline for lodging objections to the Boundaries Extension Bill was drawing near, and John Greig, the town clerk of Leith, decided to take action on his own responsibility, even before the Town Council had met to decide on the plebiscite. He had envelopes addressed to every household in Leith, and made an arrangement with a local printer to stop everything on hand at a moment's notice, clear his machines, and rush through the necessary printed voting forms. The council meeting went as he had anticipated, and on the following two days the printer delivered to the town clerk about 39,000 cards to be put in the post. These were all delivered by Monday morning; by the following Wednesday almost

The Kirkgate c.1910: A picture that lingers in the memory of old Leithers — the street which epitomised the old town.

31,000 cards had been returned, and voting closed on Friday 23rd January. The *Edinburgh Evening News* referred to this as the 'Lightning Plebiscite', and the name stuck.

The result of the voting was 5357 in favour of amalgamation with Edinburgh, 29,891 against. Despite this unequivocal rejection, the amalgamation went through, to an angry chorus from Leithers protesting and claiming that the port had been cheated. Long after the plebiscite had been forgotten in Edinburgh it was remembered with keen resentment in Leith. But the plebiscite had never been anything more than a futile gesture — a last-minute attempt to placate public opinion. The surge of protest from Leith led to a parliamentary enquiry, at which the facts of the case were clearly stated. Amalgamation had become inevitable; there was no real choice in the matter.

A number of facts concerning the plebiscite never appear to have been realised in Leith. On the Saturday after the fateful council meeting, while the voting papers were still in the post, every household in Leith received a communication:

MANIFESTO TO THE ELECTORS OF LEITH

Having learned of the Town Council's decision to take a Plebiscite on the question of Amalgamation with Edinburgh, we desire to impress upon you the extreme importance of every Elector recording his or her Vote upon this momentous occasion in the history of our Town.

185

This fresh attempt on the part of the Corporation of Edinburgh to deprive us of the right to manage our local affairs, as embodied in their Annexation Proposals, is entirely without justification, and in our considered judgment its adoption would be distinctly harmful to the best interests of the Burgh of Leith.

We have no hesitation, therefore, in urging you to answer the question on the Plebiscite Card with an unmistakeable NO.

> Richard Mackie, Ex-Provost of Leith.
> Malcolm Smith, Ex-Provost of Leith.

William Crawford, Biscuit Manufacturer.
Robert Cross, J. & J. Cunningham, Ltd.
John Garden, Garden, Haig-Scott & Wallace, W.S.
Andrew Gibson, Ex-Magistrate of Leith.
Alex. J. Lethem, John Lethem & Sons.
C. McManus, O.M.I., St. Mary's Star of the Sea, Leith.
James M. Manclark, Ex-Magistrate of Leith.
F.G. Salvesen, Chr. Salvesen & Co. Shipowners.
James M. Scott, Junction Road U.F. Church,
> Chairman, Leith Education Authority.
W.F. Stewart, Ex-Magistrate of Leith.
William Swan, South Leith Parish Church.
William Taylor, Ex-Chairman, Leith Parish Council.
William Thomson, William Thomson & Co. Ltd, Shipowners.
T.W. Tod, A. & R. Tod Ltd, Leith Flour Mills.
J.R.S. Wilson, North Leith Parish Church.
Note:— Please show this letter to all Electors in your household, or with whom you are associated in business or other ways.

The signatures following those of Sir Richard Mackie and Mr Malcolm Smith were obtained on very short notice. Had there been more time, many more names could have been easily got.

The signatures of Sir Richard Mackie and Mr (Later Sir) Malcolm Smith carried great weight, for these gentlemen were highly esteemed in the town. On the other hand, as Edinburgh protested, the voters were given no information — no facts at all — to indicate that there was any real case for amalgamation. Leith newspapers denied this, and pointed out that for months past the Edinburgh press had been full of arguments in favour of the proposed union. Placards advising electors to vote NO were extensively posted up throughout the town, and advertisements to the same effect were carried in the local press. A considerable number of canvassers also went from door to door during the week of the plebiscite. Another fact is that it was never

Protest Banner: The local press declared their interest. This banner was hung outside the office of the *Leith Observer* in Tolbooth Wynd.

explicitly stated whether the voters' roll used was the roll of local government electors, or that of parliamentary electors, which was larger, covering a wider area. From the town clerk's statement of the number of voting cards posted it would seem that the parliamentary roll was used, but the results were quoted as though the smaller local government roll had been used. One way and another the plebiscite seems to have been conducted in an improper manner, and did the cause of independent Leith no good at all.

At the parliamentary enquiry Gotfred Taylor, a civil engineer, was examined. He said 'Leith is practically at the end of its life: it cannot grow any more. It has arrived at full age and there it has got to stop for the rest of its life unless it extends into Edinburgh, or Edinburgh extends into Leith and they become one'. This put the situation in a nutshell, but on no occasion were the electors in the Plebiscite informed of the all-important fact that Leith could not extend her boundaries, as all the adjacent land had passed into the possession of Edinburgh. It is inconceivable that the Leith town councillors, or the signatories to the Manifesto, were unaware of this fact, so the information must have been deliberately withheld from the public. It is also more than likely that the knowledge that there was no real choice for Leithers in the matter of amalgamation explains the silence of Leith Town Council all through 1919. When the *Leith Observer* suggested a plebiscite, the Town Council, instead of backing the suggestion, ought to have refused it and explained the reason to the public. The editor of the *Observer*, however, must share the blame for the deception of the people of Leith, for he must certainly have known that the plebiscite could be no more than a charade.

The original culprits were the town councillors of the nineteenth century, who watched idly as Edinburgh obtained a series of Boundaries Extension Acts. The reason for their inactivity was probably financial. As we have seen, the Town Council was very hard pressed for money during its first twenty years or so. In 1854 Leith bought the Links from Edinburgh and took some years to find the money after establishing a sinking fund for the purpose. Then the slum clearance of the 1880s and the acquisition of several parks in the years following were a fresh strain on financial resources. To crown all, the proposal for amalgamation first made in 1894 came at a very bad time, for the Town Council were just then in trouble with the Hospital Managers, who were urging the immediate necessity for a separate hospital for infectious diseases, and money had to be found for the hospital that was built at East Pilton. Edinburgh got three Extension Bills through Parliament in quick succession, in 1896, 1900 and 1901, and this really sealed Leith's fate. Leith councillors at the turn of the century must have been appalled at Edinburgh's extension to Seafield and Granton. Perhaps they ought to have gone ahead with an Extension Bill of their own at that time, and taken on more consequent debt, but they decided otherwise. But from then on there was no real choice for Leith: eventual amalgamation was inevitable.

CHAPTER 12

How Goes It?

The new relationship with Edinburgh which was forced on Leith in 1920 did not have the dire consequences that had been feared. In the post-war world of the 1920s both the city and the port had changed and developed out of all recognition from the days of King William IV. The port was not absorbed into Edinburgh with the amalgamation. The community remained distinct and distinctive, just as Newhaven, although part of the parish of North Leith from 1630, had retained its distinctive atmosphere and interests — a fishing village relating to but separate from the industrialism of the seaport. Apart from the merging of public services and the addition of the residents of Leith to the voters' roll of Edinburgh, it was hard to discern any great change brought about by amalgamation. Amid the list of advantages it had been claimed would follow on union, housing and unemployment, it was suggested, would be greatly benefited. This did not happen.

Edinburgh could not achieve the impossible, and even in Leith it was recognised that 'circumstances beyond our control' was an argument that had to be accepted. Housing in Leith was as bad as anywhere in Britain, and the City Corporation did try to make inroads upon slum clearance. The remaining lands of the Earl of Moray at Lochend were acquired and the first of the Corporation housing schemes was built there from 1924 onwards, the tenants of the new houses being drawn from the Royal Mile and from Leith. At the same time demolition of the worst of the slums began, and the drift of Leithers to other countries got under way. The parallel movement of people to the housing schemes and in emigration continued like a haemorrhage for the next half-century, apart from the interruption of the Second World War. The result is that in the 1980s Leith holds less than half the population of the '20s and '30s.

The people themselves were both relieved and chagrined at their removal from the port. The light and open environment of the housing schemes was welcomed after the dark, damp and decaying old tenements, but there was a heavy price to be paid. The sense of community had gone. People were drawn from a wide area into the

Schemes, and it takes a long time to relate to strangers. Many families had lived in Leith for generations. They were known throughout the neighbourhood; their virtues and their vices, their successes and distinctions, as well as their failures and shame were common knowledge. Hardship and suffering produced in many stairs a shared life, neighbours living together as a kind of extended family, loving and arguing, fighting and celebrating together with perfect mutual understanding. All that was sloughed off in the housing schemes. But Leith was still there, and for many of those who had moved out, the weekly trip back to Leith for the family shopping became a kind of institution. Once back in the Kirkgate or Great Junction Street (always 'Junction Road' to Leithers), shopping proceeded, but it was no more than a pretext for meeting with old friends and neighbours.

The final tragedy came in the 1960s when the heart of the old town was torn out, and the Kirkgate and Toolbooth Wynd were demolished in the name of progress! It was a prime example of how a development which looks well on paper can yet be quite wrong for an area, when it is put in hand without reference to the people who have lived there and who will live there in time to come. The result was the creation of a housing scheme in the heart of the town, where for centuries there had been an intermixture of houses, shops and recreational facilities, in which small businesses in great variety had provided a many-sided area of interest to the close-knit community there. No praise was given to this development; but the complexity of the problem was not realised. Shops and trades need customers, and as houses and even whole streets in the town were at the same time being demolished, fewer and fewer customers were left to support new shops. The prevailing cry and complaint in the 1960s was that more and more houses were needed, and the pace of building was too slow. To meet this demand Leith, like other towns throughout the country, was provided with several high-rise tower blocks, which provided hundreds of small flats but also created many new problems, and were generally voted to be a mistake.

In the years following the First World War another great incubus in the life of Leith was unemployment. This had been a long-standing problem in the seaport where so much work was seasonal and intermittent. In the early years of this century the state of trade fluctuated considerably, and the annual surge of winter unemployment troubled the Town Council, and various charitable bodies, when there was no government relief. After 1918 shipbuilding fell away, and one after another the Leith yards either fell idle or merged with other firms, with the loss of many jobs. Through the inter-war years Leith remained an unemployment 'black spot'; but even so, and despite the continuing flow of emigration, there were still fully 80,000 people in the port when the Second World War began.

The aftermath of that second war was as serious for Leith as the trauma of the '20s and '30s had been. The demolition of thousands of sub-standard houses had one unfortunate consequence, in that young people marrying could not find anywhere in Leith to set up house. A whole generation was lost to the port in this way, and the community became distorted — overloaded with the elderly. Sadly bereft of the young families on whom the future of the port depended, Leith acquired the unwanted reputation of having a higher proportion of old age pensioners in the population than any other town in Scotland. Too many old-timers spent too much time lamenting the passing of the roaring, rumbustious life of the Kirkgate and the Shore they recalled from their youth. The port had fallen quiet and dour.

Unnoticed at the time, however, a change was taking place. A spark of new life was kindled which was fanned over the years into a flame which grew to become the glow of new confidence that suffuses the town today. In 1955 the countrywide mass X-ray campaign got under way in an effort to stamp out tuberculosis, and in Leith a committee drawn from a wide spectrum of public life in the town organised a door-to-door visitation to have the whole population screened. When the campaign was over the committee met for the last time, and great satisfaction was expressed over the warm co-operation between people from so many different walks of life. Would it not be possible to direct this energy and interest in other ways to benefit the town? Many of Leith's needs could only be met through the action of local and central government, but at the same time self-help might strengthen the old community spirit. One glaring fact obtruded itself as a result of the door-to-door visitation in the town; this was that a great many old people were living alone, frail and house-bound, and being cut off in this way were quite friendless, and so at risk. It was decided to organise a lunch club to bring elderly people together while they were still able to leave their homes, so that they might make new friends, who would report on each other's growing frailties, and so bring into being a kind of pensioners' community.

The resultant lunch club was the first of its kind in Scotland. From 1956 it met five days a week in premises provided by the then Leith Provident Co-operative Society. Volunteers were in attendance, but the old people themselves were actively involved from the start. Four years later the club opened its own premises, purpose-built in the yard of the former Swanfield Flour Mill, given for the benefit of the pensioners. Contributions of money, materials and labour flowed in for the provision of this building, and for the day-to-day running of the club. In 1961 Andrew Lamb's House in Burgess Street, the best-preserved example in the city of a merchant's house from the early seventeenth century, was opened as the first Old People's Day Centre in the country. Throughout Leith there was a stir of hope, a feeling that the old spirit had not yet died after all. If there were more old people in the port than anywhere else in the land, it was appropriate that Leith should be showing the way to provide for these old folk.

There were still many years of deprivation to be endured, for as the Westminster government regarded industrial Leith as only a part of non-industrial Edinburgh, the port was excluded from sharing in the 40% government development grant given to industrial communities trying to extend and modernise their factories and workplaces. The effect of this was disastrous for Leith, as many firms now arranged to leave the town and move to other places where they could benefit from the government grant. Many old names and long-established firms disappeared from Leith at that time.

The growing feeling for the value of self-help was evinced again, however, when in 1972 the Port of Leith Housing Association was formed. This body began in a tentative, experimental way to reconstruct and modernise a number of old tenements which were in danger of being demolished, as had happened in so many other cases. The modernised flats were immediately popular and successful, and the Housing Association developed rapidly. Many of the old tenements were substantial, well-proportioned buildings which lent themselves admirably to modernisation. The work of the Housing Association slowed the rate of demolition considerably, and Leithers, observing this, took fresh heart. The unsuitability of tower blocks was now apparent to the City Corporation, and several three and four-storey blocks of flats began to appear — very attractive houses, immediately and gratefully occupied. Young people marrying were

The Changed Picture: A scene impossible to imagine in former days. Since the mouth of the Water of Leith was closed by lock gates, the water is maintained at a high level. The river is no longer tidal.

now able to settle in Leith if they wished, which was a change of immense significance for the future of the port.

'What's so special about Leith?' asked the housing manager at Edinburgh City Chambers. 'We are moving people from many run-down areas of the city to the new housing schemes, and they are all only too happy to move — except the folk from Leith. Every family we move from Leith at once applies to go back again as soon as possible. Why? Leith is no beauty spot.' His mystification was understandable, for even to old Leithers the port is no longer what it was. Whole streets have disappeared, and in the main shopping areas the number of Indian and Pakistani names is very noticeable. For a time, indeed, Great Junction Street was referred to in derision as the Khyber Pass, but this name has not stuck as the Asian newcomers have quickly settled into the town, commending themselves as quiet, hard-working and well-mannered people. The bulk of the Sikh community in the city is to be found in Leith, where they established their own Temple in the former St. Thomas's Church. Over the centuries Leith has welcomed and eventually absorbed into itself a

'PERSEVERE' — *the Spirit of Leith:* Lorne Street Primary School pupils determined to master the art of using a blowpipe.

great many different peoples, as the family names to be found in the town today bear ample witness. Here are names from Orkney and Shetland, from Norway and Sweden. Families in Leith today can tell of French, German and Italian forebears, and eighteenth and nineteenth-century records refer to Negroes and Chinese; and the Eskimo John Sakehouse was brought to Leith early last century, although he was not followed by any others from that airt. In two or three generations these incomers have all made good Leithers — part of a tolerant, warmhearted people.

Many of the changes have been inevitable, and are not due to arbitrary decisions or malevolent intentions on anyone's part. To anyone who knew the docks fifty years ago the sight of the deserted quays today is depressing: but this is misleading. The advent of much larger vessels meant that deepwater facilities had to be provided by reclaiming more land, and providing berthage for these ships much further out into the channel of the Forth than the old dock area, so they are not seen by the casual stroller round the nineteenth-century docks. Bulk cargoes, containerised cargoes and automatic handling equipment have put an end to the days when eight dockers and eight

Bernard Street, Leith: Named after Bernard Lindsay, Groom of the Chamber to King James VI. This wide street of Georgian buildings replaced the old Weigh-house Wynd in the late 18th century.

stevedores were needed to deal with a cargo. The large number of men formerly employed in the grain elevators and flour mills are no longer needed for the automatic processing of bulk cargoes of grain. Yet a very large volume of business is dealt with at Leith today.

Undoubtedly the arrival of the Scottish Development Agency in Leith will come to be seen as an event of great historic importance for the port. Investing several million pounds in the town, the S.D.A. entered upon a scheme of attracting small businesses to Leith to take the place of the much larger firms that had provided the bulk of employment in former days. The removal or collapse of such large employers of labour was a very serious matter for Leith, as hundreds of jobs were lost, sometimes with little warning. Smaller firms engaged in a greater variety of work would establish a new pattern of employment and even bring a new character to the industrial life of the town. The small industrial units provided by the S.D.A. have been readily taken up by a great many new firms. Attention has also been paid to improving the appearance of the best buildings and streets in Leith, and the effect of extensive stone-cleaning is an impressive transformation in the 200-year-old commercial centre of the town in Constitution Street and Bernard Street. This, in fact, is the most extensive 18th century commercial area in Scotland to

195

remain virtually unchanged in outward appearance since the first erection of the buildings. Moreover these premises today are used for the same business pursuits as they were built to accommodate. Banks, insurance brokers, shipping offices, and various trades and shops connected with seagoing still flourish here, and in the vicinity of the Shore a metamorphosis is taking place. Along the bank of the river a walkway accompanies the Water of Leith from its mouth right up through the city. Gone is the old cluttered confusion of gear and rubbish along the harbour wall; the stinking water has been cleaned; shrubs and trees are being introduced, and the river which centuries ago was the great attraction bringing wealthy city merchants to build second homes by the beautiful Water of Leith is again coming to be seen as one of the great assets of the port. Several prestigious restaurants have been opened in the vicinity, and all the signs and portents indicate a more prosperous time for this old port than it has known for a long time past.

All this, however, does not answer the housing manager's question, Why should anyone wish to go back to Leith? The port is by no means as depressed and deprived as it was when he asked the question, but many other towns have had their ups and downs, and do not appear to exert the subtle pull that Leith does on those who have known the place. A remark by another city official perhaps indicates where the truth lies. 'My work takes me all over the city,' he said, 'and I notice that only in Leith do people speak of going to Edinburgh. Leith is part of this city, just as Newington, Corstorphine and Morningside are part of the city; but in Leith the general assumption seems to be that Edinburgh is a different place.' That's it: Leith is different. We know it, and we know it today without any animosity. There is no escaping our heritage, our history, which powerfully influences our attitudes and priorities today. Even for the resident of only a few years the sense of community is strong, so that walking the streets of Leith is walking among friends. Some are personally known and recognised; many more are strangers, but if all that is known of a stranger is that he is a Leither, that is enough to forge a link, for at once we realise many interests and feelings and ideals in common.

This book is an attempt to set on record an account of what it is that makes Leith different and special, of what it is that exerts a lifelong pull on every Leither, no matter where he or she may be settled in the world. And for the next generation at least this old port will still exert her spell, for even the youngsters leaving school in Leith today and going to work or to university very soon inform their new friends that they are Leithers. There is a special cachet, it seems, attaching to anyone who can claim connection with this great and stirring old port.

Index

Stark, Thomas, 156
Stead, John and David, 47
Steamers, 14
Stewart of Laverockbank, John, 79
Stewartfield, 130
Stirling steamship, 30
Stocking-making, 107
Straiton, Mrs, 56
Street naming, 180
Struthers, Dr James, 82
Suez Canal, 30
Sugar refining, 46
Superiority of Leith, 14, 16f., 33
Syme, John, shipbuilder, 44
Sympathetic Society, 78

Tabernacle, the, 162
Tailors, Incorporation of, 5
Tarbert, James, 152
Taylor Gardens, 96, 180
Tennant Street, 129, 178
Third Police Act, 173
Thistle Golf Club, 58, 62
Thorburn, Wm., 48
Thorburn, W.D., 114
Tolbooth Wynd, 3, 71, 76, 112
Town drummer, 74
Town Tax, 73
Trades of Leith, 36
Trafalgar Lane, 94
Trafalgar masonic lodge, 166
Trafalgar Street, 131
Traffic Regulation (Scotland) Act, 138
Traffickers, Incorporation of, 36, 41, 69, 93
Trial, The, 23f.
Trinity Free Church, 164
Trinity House, 35, 99, 102
Trustees of High School, 101, 103ff.

Udwart, Nicolas, 45
Ukrainian Church, 168
Unemployment, 95, 190f.
Unicorn, The, 12
Union Canal, 174
United Associate Church, 160

United Presbyterian churches, 164f.
Upper Drawbridge, 28
Upper Quarryholes, 117

Vaults, the, 4, 71
Vegetables, introduction of, 123
Veitch, Hugh, 130
Victoria Baths, 62
Victoria Dock, 30
Victoria Park, 180
Vulgar school, 98

Walker's school, 110
Water Street, 3, 71
Water supply, 69–74
Watt, Provost James, 82, 179
Watt's Hospital, 106
Weaponshowings, 10, 50
Wemyss, Earl of, 52
Wesley, John, 162
West India Steam Packet Co., 177
West Old Dock, 28
West Pier, 30
'Whisky money', 114
White Lion, the, 137
White, Wm., 120
Wightman, Robert, 44
Wilkie, Thomas, 156
Wilson, James, 20
Wilson, Mrs, 107
Wine trade, 4
Wishart, George, 13, 150
Wishart, John K., 113
Wishart, Rev. Wm., 154
Wishart, Rev. Wm. II, 156
'Woman's school', 106
Wood, Alexr., 57, 102
Wood, Patrick, 39
Wood, Peter, 76
Woodcock, Adam, 134f.
Wrights and Masons, Incorporation of, 5

Yardheads, 66, 158, 163
Yooll's Wharf, 1